# HITLER'S WAR MACHINE

# GERMAN PARATROOPS
# 1939-45
## The Fallschirmjäger

### EDITED AND INTRODUCED
### BY BOB CARRUTHERS

D1557575

Pen & Sword
**AVIATION**

This edition published in 2013 by
Pen & Sword Aviation
An imprint of
Pen & Sword Books Ltd
47 Church Street
Barnsley
South Yorkshire
S70 2AS

First published in Great Britain in 2012 in digital format by
Coda Books Ltd.

Copyright © Coda Books Ltd, 2012
Published under licence by Pen & Sword Books Ltd.

ISBN 978 1 78159 112 3

A CIP catalogue record for this book is
available from the British Library

Printed and bound in Great Britain by
CPI Group (UK) Ltd, Croydon, CR0 4YY

Pen & Sword Books Ltd incorporates the Imprints of Pen & Sword Aviation, Pen &
Sword Family History, Pen & Sword Maritime, Pen & Sword Military, Pen &
Sword Discovery, Pen & Sword Politics, Pen & Sword Atlas, Pen & Sword
Archaeology, Wharncliffe Local History, Wharncliffe True Crime, Wharncliffe
Transport, Pen & Sword Select, Pen & Sword Military Classics, Leo Cooper, The
Praetorian Press, Claymore Press, Remember When, Seaforth Publishing and
Frontline Publishing

For a complete list of Pen & Sword titles please contact
PEN & SWORD BOOKS LIMITED
47 Church Street, Barnsley, South Yorkshire, S70 2AS, England
E-mail: enquiries@pen-and-sword.co.uk
Website: www.pen-and-sword.co.uk

# CONTENTS

# INTRODUCTION

THIS BOOK forms part of the series entitled 'Hitler's War Machine.' The aim is to provide the reader with a varied range of materials drawn from original writings covering the strategic, operational and tactical aspects of the weapons and battles of Hitler's war. The concept behind the series is to provide the well-read and knowledgeable reader with an interesting compilation of related primary sources combined with the best of what is in the public domain to build a picture of a particular aspect of that titanic struggle.

I am pleased to report that the series has been well received and it is a pleasure to be able to bring original primary sources to the attention of an interested readership. I particularly enjoy discovering new primary sources, and I am pleased to be able to present them unadorned and unvarnished to a sophisticated audience. The primary sources such as Die Wehrmacht and Signal, speak for themselves and the readership I strive to serve is the increasingly well informed community of reader/historians which needs no editorial lead and can draw its own conclusions. I am well aware that our community is constantly striving to discover new nuggets of information, and I trust that with this volume I have managed to stimulate fresh enthusiasm and that at least some of these facts and articles will be new to you and will provoke readers to research further down these lines of investigation, and perhaps cause established views to be challenged once more. I am aware at all times in compiling these materials that our relentless pursuit of more and better historical information is at the core our common passion. I trust that this selection will contribute to that search and will help all of us to better comprehend and understand the bewildering events of the last century.

*Fallschirmjäger board transport aircraft for the invasion of Leros.*

In order to produce an interesting compilation giving a flavour of events at the tactical and operational level I have returned once more to the wartime US Intelligence series of pamphlets, which contain an intriguing series of contemporary articles on weapons and tactics. I find this series of pamphlets particularly fascinating as they are written in the present tense and, as such, provide us with a sense of what was happening at the face of battle as events unfolded.

In the 1930s Hermann Göring, after having observed Soviet airborne infantry manoeuvres, became committed to the creation of Germany's airborne infantry. He ordered the formation of a specialist police unit in 1933, devoted to protecting Nazi party officials. The unit carried out conventional police duties for the next two years, but in 1935, Göring transformed it into Germany's first dedicated airborne regiment. The unit was incorporated into the newly-formed Luftwaffe later that year and training commenced. Göring also ordered that a group of volunteers be drawn for parachute training. These volunteers would form a cadre for a future Fallschirmtruppe ("parachute troops").In January 1936, 600 men and officers formed a Jäger and an engineer company. Germany's parachute arm was officially inaugurated in 1936 with a call for recruits for a parachute training school. The school was open to Luftwaffe personnel, who were required to successfully complete six jumps in order to receive the Luftwaffe Parachutist's Badge.

During World War II, the German Air Force (Luftwaffe) raised a variety of airborne light infantry (Fallschirmjäger) units. The Luftwaffe built up a division-sized unit of three Fallschirmjäger regiments plus supporting arms and air assets, known as the 7th Flieger Division. Throughout World War II, the Fallschirmjäger commander was Kurt Student, his Fallschirmjaeger are instantly recognisable from the special version of the German armed forces' steel helmet was issued to Fallschirmjäger units.

Fallschirmjäger participated in many of the famous battles of World War II and in many theatres. As elite troops they were frequently deployed at the vanguard of attacks and as the bulwark of a difficult defence. They saw action in the Norway and Denmark campaigns and in Belgium, Holland and France in 1940. They also took part in major actions in the Balkans Campaign, Crete, Italy. They took part in the final battles for Tunisia and were prominent on both the Eastern Front and later on the Western Front serving in Normandy, Holland and the Ardennes.

The dramatic airborne seizure of Fort Eben-Emael permitted the early capture of Belgium and, alongside successful operations in Holland, was a crucial element of the disorientating speed of the German victories in 1940. The major airdrops in Norway and Denmark in May 1940 were also vital to the success of the campaigns in those countries. In common with the amphibious forces in Norway, the Fallschirmjäger suffered very heavy casualties.

The Battle of Crete in 1941 saw large-scale airdrops in which the entire 7th Air Division was deployed with the elite German 5th Mountain Division acting as the follow-up. Crete was eventually captured, after fierce fighting against Greek, Commonwealth and British forces. A famous victory was eventually achieved which, despite the escape of the bulk of the Allied forces, nonetheless brought with it the capture of a large body of enemy troops and all of their weapons, but the high casualties suffered by the Fallschirmjäger as they parachuted in to battle convinced Hitler that such mass airdrops were no longer useful in relation to the costs. From that point onwards although a number of smaller operations were attempted and the Fallschirmjäger were limited to dogged defensive operations.

They gained lasting fame in the Battle of Monte Cassino where Fallschirmjäger division held the ground near the Monastery of Monte Cassino. After the monastery had been bombed by the Allies, the Germans moved into protected positions among the rubble and cellars. The Fallschirmjäger held out for months against repeated assaults and heavy

*German paratroopers interrogating a Soviet partisan, Demyansk.*

bombardment. It was here they gained the nickname "Green Devils" from the Allied forces for their distinctive jackets and their tenacious defence. Inflicting huge losses on the Allied forces, they ultimately retreated from their positions only to avoid being outflanked.

Fallschirmjäger also played a key role defending positions in France against much larger forces in 1944, even holding on to some of the German-occupied regions until the surrender of Germany.

After mid-1944, new Fallschirmjäger recruits were no longer trained as paratroops due to the strategic situation, and from then on fought as infantrymen. A limited series of airborne operations were featured as part of the Ardennes offensive. Near the end of the war, a series of new Fallschirmjäger divisions was raised, with a corresponding reduction in quality in the later units which, however, still inflicted moderate losses on the advancing Allied troops. The last parachute division to be raised by Germany during World War II was destroyed during the Battle of Berlin in April 1945.

The style of parachute harness used by the Fallschirmjäger in World War II is generally considered inferior to those used by the British and American paratroopers. Paratroopers had to throw themselves forward out of the aeroplane, and in the resulting face-down position when the chute opened, control was nearly impossible. The necessity of landing on knees and elbows reduced the amount of equipment the trooper could carry and increased the chance of injury. As a result, they jumped armed only with a holstered pistol and a small "gravity knife". Rifles and other weapons were dropped in separate containers and, until these were recovered, the soldiers were poorly armed.

Fallschirmjäger units were usually very well equipped; they had access to the best weapons of the German military. They were among the first combat units to use assault rifles and recoilless weapons in combat. Fallschirmjäger also readily employed the best of several foreign-made small arms. The FG 42 automatic rifle, which combined the firepower of a machine gun with the lightweight handling characteristics of a standard infantry rifle, was developed specially for the paratroopers.

Thousands of German paratroops were killed in action and as a result of their outstanding bravery a total of 134 Knight's Crosses were awarded to the men of Fallschirmjäger divisions between 1940 and 1945.

Thank you for buying this volume, we hope you will enjoy discovering some new insights and will go on to try the others in the series.

*Bob Carruthers*
*Edinburgh 2012*

# ENEMY AIR-BORNE FORCES

## PREPARED BY MILITARY INTELLIGENCE SERVICE, WAR DEPARTMENT

### SPECIAL SERIES NO. 7, DECEMBER 2, 1942

## SECTION I

# INTRODUCTION

## 1. DEFINITIONS

The air forces of a nation fly and fight in the air. Airborne forces, transported to battle through the air, are primarily trained to fight on and for the ground. U.S. Army doctrine on the Tactics and Technique of Air-Borne Troops is set forth in Basic Field Manual FM 31-30, published May 20, 1942. For those unacquainted with this manual, the following official definitions may be helpful:

• *Air-Borne Troops* - any transported by air.

• *Air-Landing Troops* - troops carried in powered aircraft, or in gliders towed behind aircraft, who disembark after the aircraft or glider reaches the ground.

• *Parachute Troops* - troops moved by air transport and landed by means of parachutes.

Several other definitions, as used by United States Army Air Forces, may be quoted from Army Regulations No. 95-35, of July 7, 1942:

• *Landing field* - an area of land designated for the take-off and landing of aircraft.

• *Airdrome* - a landing field at which military facilities for shelter, supply, and repair of aircraft have been provided.

• *Air base* - a command which comprises the installations and facilities required by and provided for the operation,

*The men who were responsible for the capture of Fort Eben Emael, in the first major parachute operation of the war, May 1940.*

maintenance, repair, and supply of a specific air force.

- *Airport* - a tract of land or water which is adapted for the landing and take-off of aircraft and which provides facilities for their shelter, supply, and repair; a place used regularly for receiving or discharging passengers or cargo by air.

## 2. THE HISTORY OF THE PARACHUTE

The idea of the parachute goes back several hundred years. The first record of the use of the parachute device in an air disaster was the successful escape of a Pole, Jodaki Kuparento, from a burning balloon, July 24, 1808. From the birth of the balloon, the parachute remained mainly an exhibition medium, even to within recent years.

The first parachute jump from an airplane was demonstrated by a stunt man, Grant Morton, early in 1912, at Venice, California, from Phil Parmalee's Wright. He carried the folded parachute in his arms and threw it into the air after he jumped. The first pack-type descent was made by Bert Berry, March 1, 1912, at Jefferson Barracks, Missouri, from a Benoist plane flown by Tony Jannus. This parachute was not actually of pack type, as the parachute was stowed in a metal cone and held by break cords. The cone was tied to the front wheel skid, and a life line ran from the suspension lines inside the cone to a belt and trapeze bar, which supported Berry, who jumped from the rear axle. In the autumn of 1912, Rodman Law made many voluntary exhibition jumps with the Stevens pack, from the Wright airplane of Harry B. Brown. Charles Broadwick and Glenn Martin developed a similar type, repeatedly demonstrated by a girl, "Tiny" Broadwick, in 1913. The present Mrs. Floyd Smith made her first jump from a Martin plane with the Martin-Broadwick pack, on April 8, 1914, at 650 feet. At about the same time, "Tiny" Broadwick demonstrated the Martin-Broadwick pack to the Army's flying school at San Diego: the Chief Signal Officer, General Scriven, reported "considerable merit, warranting its development for use in our service."

The first record of parachute use in an airplane escape is the jump from a burning plane by an Austrian pilot on the Russian front in the fall of 1916, with a Heineke sack-type affair. Later, another Austrian made a forced jump from a disabled plane, and Austrian and German pilots in greater numbers began carrying such parachutes and using them for emergency escape. Both sides used parachutes in observation balloons, but no parachutes were used in airplanes by any of the Allies in World War I until after the Armistice. They had been offered to U.S. front-line aviation by our S.O.S. as early as August, 1917, but were refused by our front-line Air Force commander until after the Germans had used them successfully.

## 3. AIR-BORNE PIONEERING

The idea of air-borne troops was promulgated by Benjamin Franklin in 1784, shortly after observing the ascension of the Charles hydrogen balloon at Paris. He wrote: "Five thousand balloons, capable of raising two men each, could not cost more than five ships of the line; and where is the prince who can afford so to cover his country with troops for its defense, as that ten thousand men descending from the clouds might not in many places do an infinite deal of mischief before a force could be brought together to repel them?" Before this, even before the invention of the balloon, Friar Joseph Galien proposed that with such a vehicle it would be possible "to transport a whole army and all their munitions of war from place to place as desired." With the advent of large airplanes prior to World War I, the possibility of their use for troop transport was obvious.

During the first 2 years of World War I, intelligence agents were sometimes transported by air and landed close to special destinations behind enemy lines by the British. The possibilities of flying troops and supplies to points behind the enemy lines were actually planned by America's General "Billy" Mitchell for the 1919 Campaign. The British Handley-Pages had already been developed as the possible vehicle. The fighting ended before the bold plan could be tried out, but the proposition continued to be considered. It should be remembered also that in Russia during the years 1914-1917, Igor Sikorsky built 75 great transport planes, which were used mainly for bombing and observation but partly for transportation of personnel and matériel.

## 4. PROGRESS AFTER WORLD WAR I

Taking the lead in the development of the parachute, the United States gave the world a superior type. After the war, the Air Service continued the development of the parachute at Wright Field until definite models were established as standard. A few U.S. soldiers were instructed in the parachute and some desultory jumps were made at Kelly Field about 1920-1921. Other countries, notably the U.S.S.R., followed the American lead; and, for a time, foreign armies took the fore in air-borne development. Parachuting, as a tactical method, was first actually tried out by the Russians, who dropped their men from comparatively high altitudes with a clockwork device to open the parachutes. By 1929, newspapers and newsreels reflected the parachute-consciousness of the Soviet Army. The Germans saw the possibilities of parachuting and developed the idea of dropping men at low heights, the parachute pack being attached to the plane so that the parachute opens as the weight of the falling man pulls it out of the pack. The first military parachute troop in Germany was formed in the autumn of 1935. In 1936, 5 years before the Germans were to undertake their spectacular air invasion of Crete, Soviet maneuvers demonstrated that masses of troops could be transported by air and landed by parachute. The Italians staged mass jumps in North Africa in 1937.

In 1933 in American maneuvers in the Panama Canal Zone three batteries of 75-mm pack howitzers were flown on an emergency defensive mission, setting a major precedent for air-landing artillery. Today, as befits its tremendously expanded role as a builder of airplanes and gliders, the United States has an Air-Borne Command and is intensively training all types of air-borne troops.

## 5. THE TECHNIQUE OF GLIDING

The glider was the forerunner of the airplane as we know it today, since the first airplanes were practically gliders with power. The 1903 machine of the Wrights, with which was made the world's first controlled power flight, was their glider of 1902, redesigned and fitted with a 12-horsepower engine, and with radiator, shaft, chain, and propellers. The glider, launched from hilltop, tower, or balloon, by catapult, or drawn by horse, automobile, or boat, dates to about 1866 to the glider of Wenham, who experimented with a number of gliders, patented the original type of the present-day biplane, and more or less established the effect of aspect ratio* and other aerodynamic principles.

*A group of Fallschirmjager photographed in Oslo in June 1940 following the fall of Norway.*

Gliding, for further experiment and to some extent for sport, was continued by others. Glider clubs, which continued until World War I, were started in several cities and colleges. Orville Wright returned to Kitty Hawk, North Carolina, in 1911, and made additional experiments, in the course of which he made a free glide of 9 3/4 minutes, a record which was not beaten until 10 years later. The application of power to the glider naturally dampened interest in gliding, and the technique was not generally resumed until after World War I.

About 1920, gliding received a great stimulus in Germany and gliders were towed into the air from Wasserkuppe Mountain. From the simple glider, soaring planes, very lightly loaded, of great aspect ratio, were developed, and gliding and soaring were taken up in various countries. International contests were held on Wasserkuppe, in which American pilots participated, and later, up to the present, important contests have been held in this

* *Aspect ratio is the ratio between the span (distance from wing tip to wing tip) and the mean chord (distance from leading edge to trailing edge).*

country at Elmira, New York.

Sport flying in Germany became extraordinarily popular, the German glider flying association having over 60,000 active members by 1932. Under the Paris air agreement of 1926, withdrawing limitation on the building of German aircraft, the country built a well-developed industry by 1933. Full-time flying training began on a large-scale with Goering as Air Minister, and, in 1935, as head of the Air Force. A Government proclamation had in the meantime put the German school system at the service of aviation. The German General Staff gave its blessing to the movement to make gliding a national sport; and by the opening of World War II, Goering had 300,000 glider enthusiasts from whom he could pick potential military pilots.

# AIR-BORNE OPERATIONS IN THE PRESENT WAR

## 6. THE EARLY CAMPAIGNING OF WORLD WAR II

At the outset of the Polish campaign in 1939 the Germans may have used some of their carefully trained parachutists with disappointing results. An engagement, possibly small-scale, has been rumored, in which losses ran as high as 70 to 80 percent. If such an engagement occurred, the Germans have endeavored not to publicize it. During the Norwegian Campaign of the following year, more favorable results were attained. Several air-borne attacks with small isolated units were made, some at the cost of only minor casualties. Supplies and troops were successfully flown to Narvik and dropped by parachute to reinforce the German garrison there. But at Dombas, in central Norway, a force of about 200 German parachutists were killed or captured within a week of their appearance.

## 7. THE GERMAN INVASION OF HOLLAND AND BELGIUM

In the German invasion of the Low Countries more than 10,000 men, parachutists and air-landing infantry*, and from 350 to 400 planes are estimated to have been used in this first great German employment of air-borne troops. The principal objectives were The Hague, capital of the country; the port facilities and bridges of Rotterdam, Holland's chief commercial center; the bridges of Dordrecht and Moerdijk; and the Belgian fortress of Eben Emael, the supposedly impregnable key to the Albert Canal,

---

* One report states that "between 14,000 and 18,000 air infantry troops were utilized against Holland, Belgium, and France, May 10-20, 1940."

17

*Fallschirmjäger prepare to board their aircraft, Corinth 1941.*

Belgium's main line of defense.

Transport planes carrying the troops easily infiltrated over Dutch territory at dawn on the morning of May 10, 1940, while several bombing squadrons attacked such Dutch aviation bases as Texel, Bergen, and Schipol.

After 0500, parachutists began dropping near the assigned objectives. At Rotterdam and elsewhere they seized air terminals for later use by German air-landing troops. Key points, such as bridges and bridgeheads, were seized with success at Dordrecht and Moerdijk. At Eben Emael heavy dive bombing was followed by the arrival of parachutists and glider-borne infantry who advanced from bomb crater to crater and held their own until the arrival of motorized units, notably a reinforced battalion of engineer assault troops. The garrison was forced into surrender at noon on the day after the invasion began.

Such German successes had a direct bearing on the speed with which German arms came triumphantly to the Channel. Nevertheless, at The Hague and at such adjacent bases as Ypenburg, Valkenburg, and Ockenburg, the German air-borne forces were decisively repulsed. In other scattered places, too, most of the German parachutists who landed to accomplish specific missions were either killed or captured. Also, Dutch pursuit planes and anti-aircraft guns took a slight toll of German aircraft. At some places the Dutch attacked transport planes with field pieces and machine guns; and elsewhere, mines or trenches caused the landing aircraft to crash before air infantry could be unloaded.

The German operations in Holland taught the lesson that complete air-borne success can be attained only with complete surprise. This was a lesson that was later to be emphasized at Crete.

## 8. THE CONQUEST OF FRANCE

After entering Holland and Belgium, the Germans completed their conquest of France in short order. They made no appreciable use of parachutists or other air-borne troops, possibly because they were achieving rapid successes with their air-supported ground troops. German mechanized spearheads frequently performed services in the French rear that might have been otherwise unobtainable except with the use of air-borne surprise. The impression prevails that the Germans did drop a certain number of individual parachutists disguised as civilians behind the French lines, but it is difficult to verify this alleged augmentation of the Fifth Columnists, or to establish it as a matter of any military consequence.

## 9. AIR-BORNE ATTACK AT THE BRIDGE OVER THE CORINTH CANAL

One feature of the Balkan Campaign of 1941 was a German air-borne attack in the vicinity of Corinth, Greece. On the morning of April 26, 1941, when the attack began, only a few Allied officers and men were defending the important bridge over the Corinth Canal, a ship canal which cuts through a narrow point of the rocky Grecian peninsula. The bridge had been prepared for demolition, but was being reserved intact so that withdrawing Allied troops might cross safely from the northern to the southern bank of the cut.

At 0700 the German Air Force began an intensive low-level bombing assault, directed mainly against British anti-aircraft defenses over an area a mile in radius from either side of the bridge. This action was supplemented at 0720 by extremely heavy low-level machine-gun and cannon attack from fighter aircraft. At 0740, Ju-52 troop-carrying planes, some as low as 200 feet, appeared, and parachutes began to drop. Several hundred parachutists - the exact number is somewhat uncertain - followed by parachuted containers and unparachuted containers, were dropped over the canal area in previously selected positions in a matter of 30 minutes. To prevent aid from being sent from Nablion-Argos, 20 to 30 miles south of Corinth, German fighters prohibited movement on the Corinth road, and kept up their strafing and machine-gunning intensively after the parachutists had landed.

The defenders of the bridge fired with some effect, but it was soon evident that the parachutists were taking up stations to cover each end of the bridge and thus deny its use to the British. At this juncture a British officer succeeded in setting off the prepared charge, and the bridge was destroyed. But though the Germans were balked in their attempt to seize the bridge, the site of the crossing remained in their hands.

## 10. AIR-BORNE TROOPS IN THE BATTLE OF CRETE

On May 20, 1941, the German Army launched against the Island of Crete an attack on an unprecedented scale by air-borne forces, consisting of nearly 800 bombers and fighters, 500 to 650 transport planes, and 75 gliders. The RAF could give no opposition. The 37,500 British and Greek ground troops had to contend, unaided, against about 35,000 German air-borne troops, backed by overwhelming air support. The attack began with a heavy dive-bombing raid, which was closely followed by parachute landings at Malemé, at Candia (also called Heraklion), and at Retymno and Canea. At Malemé, parachute and air-landing troops, aided by the diversionary effect of those landed elsewhere, captured the airport and cleared the way for a steady stream of air-borne reinforcements from German bases in Greece. About 60 to 80 percent of the attacking parachute troops were killed, but because the British lacked any air power whatever, they were unable to check the flow of planes and gliders. German troops continued to swarm into the island, and finally the British were forced to evacuate.

## a. Preparatory Phases

The preparation prior to the air-borne attack was divided into three distinct phases:

*The First Phase, May 1-10:* Extensive reconnaissance, primarily photographic, accompanied by light dive-bombing and machine-gunning attacks, was carried out for about 10 days.

*The Second Phase, May 10-17:* This was made up of daylight bombing and machine-gunning attacks on an ever-increasing scale, both in frequency and intensity. Thrusts were made at communications, and probing attacks to locate anti-aircraft, troop concentrations, and defensive positions.

*The Third Phase, May 17-19:* Intensified bombings were made in an effort to interrupt supplies and reinforcements, and to affect morale. Airdromes were heavily and frequently bombed and machine-gunned. German observers made daily air reconnaissance to obtain photographs, in order to study the defensive dispositions of troops and the locations of guns and slit trenches.

## b. Beginning of the Actual Attack, May 20-22

As soon as the thorough reconnaissance was completed and the supply lines had been broken and resistance battered, the air-borne troops were ready to attack. At the beginning of the attack, shortly after dawn, the bombardment of the key objective area, which was Malemé airdrome, took place. This was to silence anti-aircraft batteries and to prevent the use of roads leading to the airdrome.

### c. Landing of Glider-Borne and Parachute Troops

Immediately following this attack, gliders were landed in the area. Directly following the gliders, transports circled the airdrome and the parachute troops were dropped in waves of about 600 each. Positions which could not be overcome by the parachutists were indicated by flares and were then attacked by dive-bombing and machine-gunning.

### d. Exploitation by Air-Landing Troops, May 23-31

Even before the defenses had been thoroughly broken, troop transports were landed carrying air-infantry troops, mountain units, and auxiliaries, such as motorcycle detachments. After the key objective area was taken and strengthened, parachutists were dropped in other areas and then the troops were spread out from one area to the next in order to make contact and increase the hold. After the establishment of such areas, new objectives were attacked in the same manner and eventually contact was made between each sector.

## 11. OTHER USES OF GERMAN PARACHUTISTS

During the Russian campaign, German parachutists have been employed at various points as infantry units and engineers in order to obtain combat training and experience. Casualties are said to have been high. Parachutists have been used with Marshal Rommel's Afrika Korps in North Africa. Such troops are always a potential air-borne menace to an opposing force.

# GERMAN PARACHUTE TROOPS

## 12. HISTORICAL NOTE

During raids on large tenement districts outside Berlin in the autumn of 1933, Nazi police officers are said to have found that they could make surprise raids better by parachute than by road vehicle. The Russians, to be sure, had already shown the way to mass parachuting. A military parachute troop, as mentioned above, was formed in Germany in the autumn of 1935. In the following year, an experimental staff at Rechlin was conducting serious experiments with parachute troops, commanded by the then Brigadier General Kurt Student. Then aged about 45, he had fought in both the German Army and the German Air Force during World War I and later had been an infantry officer in the "100,000 Army"; subsequently he had been one of the leading personalities in the creation of the new German Air Force.

About 1936, from the General Goering Regiment was formed the German 1st Parachute Regiment, which had its headquarters at Stendal, 60 miles west of Berlin. By 1939 the three battalions of this regiment were expanded into regiments and along with the 7th Signal Battalion became the component elements of the 7th Air-Borne Division, called the 7th Air Division by the British.

Serving as the divisional commander, Brigadier General Student was promoted to be Major General early in 1940, the year that the Division's regiments and battalions, operating individually rather than collectively, saw service in Holland, Belgium, and Norway. In Crete, the 7th Air-Borne Division operated as the main element of the XIth Air-Borne Corps, and by the end of May 1940 Student was a Lieutenant General.

## 13. ORGANIZATION OF THE PARACHUTE REGIMENT

The regiment is the normal unit for the tactical employment of German parachute troops. Each regiment is divided into three battalions, and each battalion into three rifle or light companies and one heavy weapons company (machine-gun and mortar company). Special armament, consisting of 75-mm infantry guns and 37-mm antitank guns, is provided in the regiment for two special companies which by analogy with American nomenclature may be called the cannon company and the antitank company. The organization of the German parachute regiment is said to have been mainly determined by the carrying capacity of the JU-52, the airplane ordinarily used in transporting parachute troops. The men are usually moved by units, a platoon of 36 men being transported in a flight (Kette) of 3 planes.

## 14. ORGANIZATION CHARTS

Figures 1, 2, and 3 on the next pages show what is believed to be the approximate organization, strength, and armament of the German parachute rifle regiment, rifle company, and heavy weapons company, respectively. Variations, of course, are to be expected.

## 15. TRAINING OF GERMAN PARACHUTISTS

German parachutists (Fallschirmjaeger) are members of the Air Force who have met high physical requirements and have completed a rigorous course in one of the several large jumping schools, which are under the command of Brigadier General Ramcke. Jumping School No. 1, at Stendal, is said to have closed in December 1940; No. 2, at Wittstock, 55 miles northwest of Berlin, still exists; No. 3, at Braunschweig, 120 miles west of Berlin is said to have closed about March 1942; what is called Maubeuge Jumping School opened about January 1942 in the neighborhood of Paris, France. Each active school is said to graduate between 1,000 and 1,500 trainees a month, who then

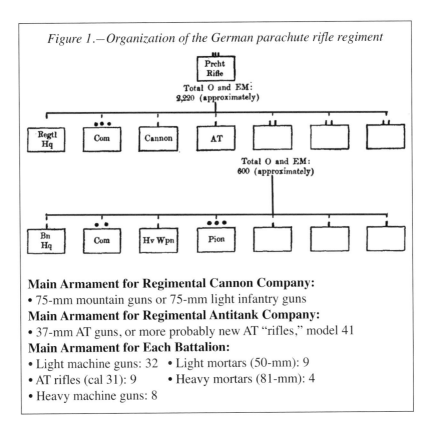

*Figure 1.—Organization of the German parachute rifle regiment*

**Main Armament for Regimental Cannon Company:**
• 75-mm mountain guns or 75-mm light infantry guns
**Main Armament for Regimental Antitank Company:**
• 37-mm AT guns, or more probably new AT "rifles," model 41
**Main Armament for Each Battalion:**
• Light machine guns: 32    • Light mortars (50-mm): 9
• AT rifles (cal 31): 9       • Heavy mortars (81-mm): 4
• Heavy machine guns: 8

normally return to their original units. Parachute school graduates, especially selected for toughness, are given further specialized training in assault tactics and assigned to assault or parachute regiments. In the spring of 1941, great attention was suddenly placed on an immediate increase in parachute troops. Numerous officers, who had seen action on the Western Front, reported to advanced instructors' schools. Training was given both in open and rugged or mountainous country, and in dropping of equipment and supplies in flights both day and night. It is estimated that more than 50,000 soldiers of the German Army now wear the diving-eagle badge of the trained parachute trooper. In each parachutist is instilled a high esprit de corps; he is taught that parachute troops perform a very important function.

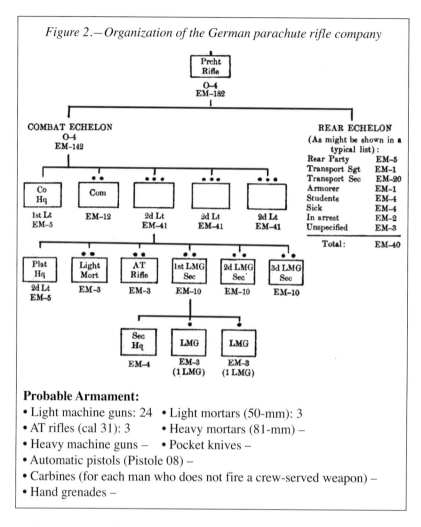

Figure 2.—Organization of the German parachute rifle company

**Probable Armament:**
- Light machine guns: 24    • Light mortars (50-mm): 3
- AT rifles (cal 31): 3         • Heavy mortars (81-mm) –
- Heavy machine guns –     • Pocket knives –
- Automatic pistols (Pistole 08) –
- Carbines (for each man who does not fire a crew-served weapon) –
- Hand grenades –

## a. Progressive Training Program

The training program is divided into ground and air phases. Recruits begin their course by learning to fall on the ground without injuring themselves. Next they learn to use the parachute harness in practice jumps at a low height from the doors of dummy airplanes. Then they are taught how to control their parachutes in the air by being suspended in their harnesses from a pulley-operated training arrangement. They are also taught to disengage themselves quickly from the parachutes as soon as they have landed. Very definite details about the training of one

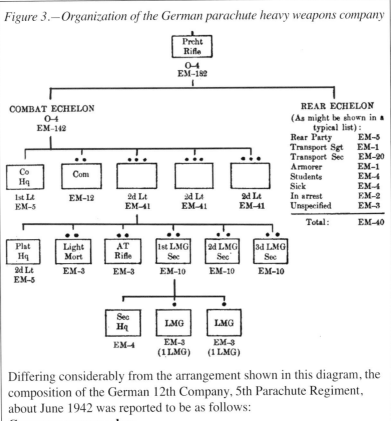

*Figure 3.—Organization of the German parachute heavy weapons company*

Differing considerably from the arrangement shown in this diagram, the composition of the German 12th Company, 5th Parachute Regiment, about June 1942 was reported to be as follows:

**Company commander:**
• 1 1st Lt

**Company headquarters:**
• 1 master sergeant (in command)    • 8 runners
• 10 engineers                                 • 7 AT riflemen

**Three identical platoons, each platoon consisting of:**
• 1 Headquarters (1 platoon leader, 3 runners, and 3 LMG gunners)
• 1 Section armed with 1 LMG (1 section leader, 1 2d-in-Comd, 10 men)
• 1 Section (of similar strength and armament to the foregoing)
• 1 Section armed with 1 Hv Mort (1 section leader, 1 2d-in-Comd, 10 men)

of the men of the German 5th Parachute Regiment are given in Appendix A.

## b. Care and Packing of Parachutes

One of the most important features of the ground phase is the course in the care and packing of parachutes. Each trooper is made personally responsible for his own equipment, and no man

*A Fallschirmjäger motorcycle messenger passes a Tiger tank in Tunisia during 1943.*

jumps unless in a parachute packed by himself. (In this, as in many other aspects of their training, the Germans are not ahead of U.S. practice.)

### c. Jumping Requirements

Having mastered the ground instructions, the pupil begins the air phase. This consists of 6 jumps, the first of which he makes alone from an altitude of about 600 feet. His next 2 jumps are made in company with 4 or 5 other trainees from an altitude of 450 feet. The fourth jump is made from this same altitude with about 10 other students, either at dawn or sunset in order to experience the light conditions of an actual attack. The fifth jump is made in combat teams of 10, each team being carried in one of 3 aircraft flying in formation. The sixth and final jump is made under simulated combat conditions from 9 aircraft flying in formation at altitudes slightly below 400 feet.

### d. Training for Ground Combat

German parachutists receive thorough ground combat training. Their individual instruction includes such subjects as marksmanship, scouting, and mechanical training on weapons. Their unit training emphasizes combat problems, demolition work, and strenuous field exercises. The training of German parachutists for ground combat resembles in many respects that given by the British to their commando units. Parachute units, of course, must practice extensively with air units, and occasionally with air-landing units.

### e. Possibility of Special Sabotage Training

The captured documents relating to the attack against Crete do not indicate that German air-borne troops were expected to commit sabotage in the true sense of the word. Damage was to be inflicted, but prisoners maintained that they had not been trained to wear, and would not wear, foreign uniforms. It has been pointed out, however, that there may well be a separate German organization for the dropping of small parties of parachute troops, possibly speaking foreign languages and wearing foreign uniforms, to create confusion, conduct sabotage, and contact fifth columnists. If so, these "parachutists" should be distinguished from the parachute regiments, which are used for large-scale open attack on important military positions.

## 16. UNIFORM AND EQUIPMENT OF GERMAN PARACHUTE TROOPS

The parachute rifleman, as a member of the German Air Force possesses an ordinary German Air Force uniform. This uniform has yellow collar patches (except possibly in the case of some specialists) and the name of the regiment embroidered on the cuff, but this is taken off before the soldier leaves the home station of the regiment. In action only the jacket of this uniform is worn, though the garrison (overseas) cap is also taken. The remainder of the combat uniform is peculiar to parachute troops.

### a. Trousers

These are like skiing trousers, quite long and loose, and gray in color. They have buttoned pockets on the sides of the thighs in which such articles as garrison (overseas) caps and swastika flags are kept.

*Fallschirmjäger on the advance during the invasion of Crete.*

### b. Helmet

This is round in shape, and is thickly padded with rubber, with a narrow brim and practically no neck-shield. It is varnished a matt blue-gray, or mottled, color, and bears ordinary German Air Force insignia. The strap forks below the ear, and is attached to the helmet at four points. The helmet is commonly worn with a cloth cover, frequently with a light-colored cross on top (the purpose of which is unknown) and with a band round it for insertion of camouflage; the band may be colored for purposes of recognition.

### c. Coveralls

This garment is of waterproof gabardine, loose fitting and fastened by a zipper fastener up the front. The color is normally olive green (or gray-green), now usually mottled. The legs are cut short some distance above the knee; the sleeves are long and button at the wrist. On both sleeves are worn large-size "wings" as stripes of rank; on the right breast is the German Air Force flying eagle (Hoheitszeichen). There are two very capacious pockets on the thighs, two more on the chest, and slits at each hip; pockets are closed by zipper fasteners. The coveralls are worn over uniform and equipment for the jump; on landing, the garment is taken off and usually put on again under the equipment.

### d. Gloves

These are of padded leather, with long gauntlets which grip by means of elastic; sometimes woolen gloves are substituted. They are worn only for the jump.

### e. Boots

These are of heavy leather, and have thick rubber soles with a V-pattern tread. They are laced up the side, and there is a seam up the front. They extend some way above the ankle, and the trousers are tucked into them; the tops fit tightly.

### f. Knee Protectors

These are of rubber, in thick horizontal bars, rather like those which some U.S. basketball players wear. They are strapped on over the trouser knee, and are discarded after the jump.

### g. Ankle Bandages

These are of linen, and are bound around instep and ankle, and about one-third of the way up the leg. The heel is left free, and the bandages are not removed after the jump.

### h. Gas Mask

Of normal type, this is carried in a special canvas container. The new gas mask (Gasmaske 40) is made of pure and very strong rubber. An antigas cape of oilcloth is also taken.

### i. Identifications

The parachutist's badge, worn low on the left breast, is a diving eagle, golden-colored, in a wreath of oak and bay of oxidized silver color; the eagle holds a swastika in its claws. (The German Army parachutist's badge is slightly different.) This badge is not worn except at home stations. An identity disc is carried; but pay-books (Soldbücher) are handed in on leaving home stations, and a camouflaged identity card (Tarnausweis or Feind-flugausweis) is taken instead.

### j. Parachutes

Types RZ16, RZ1, or 36DS28 are known. Type RZ16 -

Rückenfallschirm Zwangsauslösung 16 (back-pack, compulsion-opening parachute, type 16)-—since the beginning of 1941 has been replacing the RZ1, which opens sometimes with a dangerous jerk. The RZ16, because of its ingenious construction, opens without shock, and its opening is said to be 100 percent sure. The parachutes used in jumping schools are pure silk and are valued at 1,000 marks apiece; but the combat parachutes, intended for use only once, are made of artificial silk, or "macoo." The suspension lines are drawn together a few feet above the belt of the parachutist's harness, to the back of which they are attached by two hemp harness cords; in the air, the man seems to dangle from a single string. With the airplane traveling at 80 to 100 miles per hour, the standard height of drop is just under 400 feet. After a clear drop of about 80 feet, the parachute takes over and the subsequent rate of descent is 16 to 17 feet per second (11 miles per hour). Reports on colored parachutes are various - black, white or beige, brown, and green are all used; the principal purpose seems to be ease of recognition, though there may be some small camouflage effect against the ground (but not against the sky). A more technical description of the German parachute is given below in Appendix C.

### k. Individual Weapons

The combat pistol (Kampfpistole) is a kind of 25-mm (about 1-inch caliber) Very pistol (Leuchtspistole), but the barrel is rifled. Besides a signal cartridge, a special cartridge can be fired containing as projectile a light metal cylinder filled with scrap iron mixed with an inflammable, corrosive substance. The weapon has a strong recoil, and for that reason must be fired with both hands. The best range is about 55 yards, and bursts from the exploding projectile cover a radius of about 20 yards.

The automatic pistol 40 is a 35-caliber (9-mm) weapon with a length of about 20 inches. The sights, fixed at 110 yards, are adjustable to twice that distance. The 32-cartridge magazine functions poorly if filled with more than 24 cartridges. A good marksman can effectively fire in practice only about 4 charges of 24 cartridges per minute, though the pistol is said to have a decidedly higher rate of theoretical fire.

For the jump, the parachutist formerly carried only a large jackknife and an automatic pistol (Pistole 08) with two magazines. Men in the first platoons to land, however, might carry up to four hand grenades, and about one man in four of them a machine carbine. Since the end of March 1942, German parachutists have been required to jump with this latter weapon. Other weapons come down in weapon containers attached to "load parachutes." Experiments are being encouraged in which the individual is dropped with what he is normally equipped when operating in his combat section.

## l. Rations

Rations taken, including those in the arms containers, may last German parachutists for 2 or even 3 days. Further supplies are dropped in "provisions bombs," which are described below. Special foods taken include Wittler bread, sliced and wrapped, which is supposed to last indefinitely until unwrapped (but, in fact, does not); chocolate mixed with kola (Schokokola), and with caffeine (Kobona), which is not believed to be any better than ordinary chocolate; and simple refreshing foods like grape sugar. Most of the food is quite ordinary.

## m. Drugs and First-Aid Supplies

Parachute troops are not doped. But the following "drugs" are used: (1) energen or dextro-energen, in white tablets, a dextrose or glucose preparation, to produce energy; (2) pervitin, a drug allied to benzedrine, to produce wakefulness and alertness. Pervitin is said to create thirstiness.

The parachutist usually carries one large and two small field dressings. Each platoon has a noncommissioned officer as its medical aid man. The first-aid kit, with which he probably jumps, contains bandages, dressings, adhesive tape, safety pins, soap, ointments, iodine, antiseptics, and analgesics. Containers dropped by separate parachute have sometimes been found to hold small suitcases of extra medical supplies and surgical instruments. Each combat company has a stretcher. Since the rate of casualties may be high, the XIth Air-Borne Corps has four medical companies, one of which is probably an air-landing field hospital company. Ju-52's, which will carry eight lying casualties, may be utilized to evacuate the severely wounded to Germany.

## n. Arms Containers

Such equipment as the parachutists do not carry in the jump may be dropped in containers. Four standard arms containers are carried in each Ju-52. Each container weighs 50 to 60 pounds empty and takes a load of up to 260 pounds. Three different models have been identified: (1) a cylindrical container 5 feet long and 16 to 18 inches in diameter, hinged along its length so that it can be opened in half; (2) a container of the same length but of square cross-section, 16 inches by 16 inches, with beveled edges and hinged along its length so that one long side opens as a lid; (3) a container similar to the preceding but hinged along one long edge so that it opens in half like a trombone case. This is probably an improved design. All three of these containers are dropped in a similar manner. They are painted in various bright colors, with rings and other markings denoting the unit for which intended. Some containers have been described as fibre trunks 6 by 1½ by 1½ feet. Further details are given below in Appendix D.

## o. Contents of Arms Containers

Heavy mortars, weighing 125 pounds, and other equipment of the heavy weapons company would undoubtedly go into arms containers. Explosives of all kinds are taken, including AT and antipersonnel mines. Radio equipment goes into containers that are specially padded. Among miscellaneous articles that have been dropped by the container method have been antigas protective clothing, and particularly tools and spare parts, such as spark plugs, useful in operating commandeered motor vehicles.

### p. "Provisions Bombs" (Versorgungsbomben)

These are carried in bomb racks and released like ordinary bombs, which they resemble in shape. Any bomber aircraft may be expected to drop them on positions where troops have been landed some time previously. The "bomb" is about 6 feet in length and 1½ feet in diameter, having a separate compartment at the end to contain the parachute. On release of the "bomb," this end cap is torn off and the parachute is pulled out. There is no shock absorber. On suitable ground and from a low altitude, "provisions bombs" may be dropped without parachutes. Even ordinary sacks of provisions are so dropped.

### q. Heavy Equipment Dropped by Parachute

Much heavy parachute-borne equipment may be thrown out the door of the Ju-52, with or without a special container. Bicycles, stretchers, small flame-throwers, mines, large mortars, light artillery pieces, and perhaps motorcycles may be dropped. The 28/20-mm AT gun, model 41,* has been dropped complete and ready for action, on wheels, in a container. There is no reason why a number of other weapons could not similarly be dropped complete. In most cases they are suitable for separation into several loads, but vital time may be saved by dropping them complete. The use of several parachutes together, common in the past, has sometimes proved unsatisfactory; large parachutes are therefore being made which will take loads up to 500 pounds.

*This weapon, employing the Guerlich, or "squeeze" principle, is 28 mm at the breech and 20 mm at the muzzle.*

## SECTION IV

# GERMAN GLIDER-BORNE DEVELOPMENTS

## 17. THE COMBAT EMPLOYMENT OF GLIDER-BORNE TROOPS

In warfare the advantage of the glider over the airplane is its more silent arrival at an objective. Using the DFS 230 Glider, the Germans landed a few glider-borne troops at the Albert Canal and Fort Eben Emael in 1940. Such troops were previously in readiness during the invasion of Norway, but whether they were actually flown to combat in Norway is debatable. After Belgium fell, the Germans pushed their glider-training program. In January 1941 the partly glider-borne unit, 1st Assault Regiment (Sturmregiment 1), was created; and the corresponding towing unit of Ju-52's, the 1st Air-Landing Group (Luftlandegeschwader 1), was probably created about the same time. Both of these organizations saw service at Corinth and in Crete. The father of German military glider training is said to have been Brigadier General Ramcke, who in mid-1942 was still a leading figure in German air-borne development.

## 18. THE 1ST ASSAULT REGIMENT

The 1st Assault Regiment seems, to have been an experimental unit, designed to be the spearhead of an air-borne attack. Although the assault regiment (fig. 4) constituted somewhat like an ordinary parachute regiment, it has not only graduate parachutists but also glider pilots among its personnel. In Crete only two of its companies landed near Allied troops, both being in gliders; but the remainder of the regiment was probably at least in part landed in Ju-52's, or even dropped by parachute (though not from gliders). It is believed that only about 50

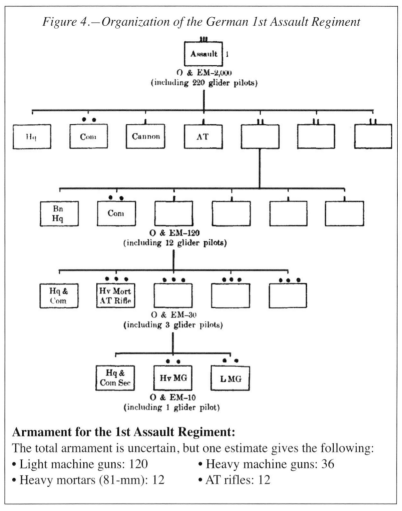

Figure 4.—Organization of the German 1st Assault Regiment

Assault 1

O & EM–2,000
(including 220 glider pilots)

Hq    Com    Cannon    AT

Bn Hq    Com

O & EM–120
(including 12 glider pilots)

Hq & Com    Hv Mort AT Rifle

O & EM–30
(including 3 glider pilots)

Hq & Com Sec    Hv MG    L MG

O & EM–10
(including 1 glider pilot)

**Armament for the 1st Assault Regiment:**
The total armament is uncertain, but one estimate gives the following:
- Light machine guns: 120
- Heavy machine guns: 36
- Heavy mortars (81-mm): 12
- AT rifles: 12

gliders may have been used. Each glider carried a single combat group with all its armament. In theory the sections of the regiment transported by gliders could immediately make ready their arms and large quantities of ammunition and explosives, and could on account of this facility pass to serious attack in very little time. Although all the men carried by glider were graduate parachutists, only the glider pilot carried a parachute. Fatalities were high because a number of gliders were hit by AA fire and fell in flames. The supposition that the 1st Assault Regiment was an experimental regiment is borne out by the fact that Brigadier

*Fallschirmjäger capture New Zealand troops during the battle for Crete.*

General Ramcke took command during the campaign in Crete, whereas the regiment was commanded both before and again after the campaign by Brigadier General Meindl.

# 19. EXPERIMENTATION WITH MILITARY GLIDERS

After the Cretan episode, experiments in the glider transport of large numbers of troops into simulated enemy territory were begun at the Experimental Department (Versuchsabteilung) of Berlin. With promise of success, the experiments were continued and intensified on the airfields of Stendal and of Lager Linde near Grossborn. In mid-1942, secret experimentation with gliders carrying as many as 50 or more men were being conducted officially on the airfields of Stendal, Hildesheim, Halberstadt, Hanover, and Berlin. Tests in carrying all-purpose vehicles and tanks have been frequent.

# 20. GLIDER-BORNE PERSONNEL

All glider pilots and glider-borne troops and the 1st Assault Regiment are members of the German Air Force, though they may initially have been in the Army. Glider pilots are generally men who have had previous civilian experience in glider flying.

But comparatively excellent civilian glider experience is said to be insufficient to qualify a pilot for operating a freight-carrying model. Training on the large gliders is done in the glider unit itself. An important feature is the making of spot landings, and blind flying is also taught. At the glider training school at Braunschweig-Waggum, the course lasts 6 weeks. No reserve pilot is carried in operations with the small glider. Air-landing troops do not necessarily have to have any special training beyond instruction and practice in getting out of the glider quickly.

# 21. THE DFS-230 GLIDER

The glider used by the Germans in Crete was a high-wing 10-seater monoplane. It is known as the DFS-230 freight-carrying glider (Lastensegler or Lastensegelflugzeug, abbreviated L.S.). It has probably been in production since the spring of 1940, and in quantity production since autumn of that year. In the spring of 1942, a minimum estimate of the number on hand was 700.

## a. Construction

It is believed that the fuselage is of tubular steel construction, and that the wings are made entirely of wood. Usually the glider's wheels have been jettisoned after take-off, the glider landing on its skid.

## b. Seating Arrangements

The interior arrangements are not spacious. The seats are in a single line, six facing forward and four backward. The four rear seats can be taken out to provide more space for freight. The DFS-230 is designed to carry a pilot and 9 men, with equipment. For rapid exit from the glider, each end is fitted with a door.

## c. Dimensions

The approximate dimensions of the DFS-230 are given as follows: span, 72 feet; length, 36 feet.

## d. Weight and Load Statistics

Various weights, according to various uses made of the glider, are as follows (in pounds):

| Weight empty, including fixed equipment | 1,818 | 1,818 | 1,818 |
|---|---|---|---|
| Useful load | 2,371 | 2,485 | 2,433 |
| Gross weight | 4,189 | 4,305 | 4,251 |

### e. Equipment

Instruments are phosphorescent, and include air speed indicator, altimeter, rate-of-climb indicator, turn-and-bank indicator, and compass. A 24-volt storage battery is fitted in the nose to operate navigation lights, cabin lights, and a landing light, which is under the port wing. A fixed light machine gun (LMG 34) is said to be attached externally to the starboard side, and is fired by the man in No. 2 seat (sitting behind the pilot), through a slit in the fuselage, as the glider is landing. Aiming of the machine gun is not possible.

### f. Towing Planes

Under combat conditions, the Ju-52 aircraft, which is ordinarily used to tow the DFS-230 glider, normally flies empty. This is because the towing plane does not fly over the objective, but releases the gliders, each of which is attached to it directly, in V-formation: glider "trains" are not used. In operations, normally one glider is towed: three Ju-52's with their gliders, fly in formation. Types such as the Me-110 or He-111 are quite suitable for use as towing aircraft. In training, and probably also for freight-carrying in rear areas, other aircraft are used for towing, including the He-45 and He-46 (training aircraft) and the Henschel-126 (army cooperation aircraft). Fighter planes have also been used to tow gliders in training. A table of tug and glider performances is given in figure 5.

### g. Length of Tow-Rope

Tow-ropes are of varying length, 40, 60, 100, or 120 yards, according to the airfield space available. The glider handles better with a longer rope. Runways are ideal for the take-off, but are not essential.

### h. Towing Distances

The distances for which the glider can be towed depend upon the range of the aircraft and the weather conditions. With extra fuel, a Ju-52 can tow a DFS-230 more than 1,000 miles.

### i. Gliding Distances

The distances which the glider can cover after release from the towing plane are variable, and depend upon such factors as windspeed, altitude of release, direction of wind relative to line of flight, navigation errors, and evasive action. In the attack on Crete gliders are thought to have been released at no more than 2 to 5 miles from shore, and at heights of not more than 5,000 feet.

### j. Table of Glider Speeds

- Towing speed: 105 mph
- Optimum gliding speed: 71.4 mph
- Holding-off speed: 55 mph
- Landing speed: 35-40 mph

### k. Landing Area

The DFS-230 glider requires only a small landing area. It has been noted that flaps may be used to steepen the angle of glide. If the skid is wound with barbed wire, or fitted with arresting hooks, landing in an even smaller area is practicable.

## 22. THE GOTHA 242 GLIDER

The Gotha 242 Glider, larger than the DFS-230, is used for troop transport in training and for freight-carrying. Six of them were captured partially destroyed at Derna. The flying characteristics are said to be such that any pilot can handle one with ease, either towed or solo. Steep turns, nevertheless, are to be avoided, and acrobatics are forbidden. Recent photographic reconnaissance has identified two powered types, experimentally equipped, respectively, with twin air-cooled radial, and twin in-line, engines.

### a. Construction

The Gotha 242 is a twin-boom monoplane, with fuselage of

*A group of Fallschirmjäger aboard a divisional half-track.*

tubular metal construction, and wings, tail boom, and tail unit made of wood. Landing is effected on three skids or on wheels, the latter of which can be jettisoned. Some of these gliders are said to have retractable landing gear. The central fuselage (37 feet long) is detachable, and is also hinged at the top, forward of the trailing edge of the wing, on which hinge the rear portion lifts upwards, making an opening 7 feet by 6 feet for loading by means of ramps which are carried in the aircraft.

## b. Dimensions

The Gotha 242 has a span of 79 feet and a length of 52½ feet.

## c. Crew and Armament

This glider carries two pilots. Control is dual, and the first pilot's seat is fully armored to a thickness of from one-tenth to three-tenths of an inch. Four light machine guns are fitted, two firing forward from the nose, and two firing aft; four more may be fitted in lateral positions.

### d. Equipment

Instruments are more numerous than in the DFS-230 and include a telephone for communication with the towing aircraft, activated, with the remainder of the electrical installation, by a 24-volt storage battery. A landing light is fitted underneath the port wing. Two first-aid kits are carried, and a ballast container capable of holding up to 925 pounds. Ballast is used only when the glider is empty.

### e. Seating Arrangements

When fitted with seats, the Gotha 242 holds 21 fully equipped men in addition to the 2 pilots.

### f. Weight and Load Statistics

The empty weight of this glider, with fixed equipment, is 7,168 pounds. The gross weight is 12,750 pounds, leaving a useful load of 5,582 pounds. Freight storage space is 20 by 8 by 6½ feet.

### g. Towing

The Gotha 242 is normally towed by one Ju-52, by means of a steel cable 80 to 300 yards long. An arrester gear may be fitted to shorten the landing run.

### h. Table of Glider Speeds

Maximum towing speed: 149 mph

Maximum gliding speed: 180 mph

Minimum gliding speed (when landing fully loaded): 87 mph

## 23. OTHER TYPES OF GERMAN GLIDERS

Besides the DFS-230 and the Gotha 242, other types of gliders have been tried out by the Germans. Three less known types are mentioned to show that glider-development in Germany seems to be tending toward more capacious models.

### a. The Merseburg Glider

A more or less experimental type of glider, the Merseburg is said to have a span of about 175 feet and a length of 94 feet. Its load might theoretically be over 20,000 pounds, but is probably less; one Ju-52 could not tow it, if the load were so high. Towing by two or three aircraft is, however, technically possible. The Merseburg glider, with a fuselage breadth of 9 to 10 feet, is wide enough to take the 9-ton tank, Pz. Kw. II. The number of troops which can be accommodated is probably from 40 to 50.

## b. The Goliath Glider

Reports have been received of a glider, perhaps known appropriately as the "Goliath," with a twin fuselage and a wing span of about 270 feet. The load is said to be 16 tons, or 140 men. Another calculation gives the possible useful load as 35,000 to 40,000 pounds, with a gross weight as high as 80,000 to 90,000 pounds. Though these reports are unconfirmed, the technical difficulties in building such a glider are not considered insuperable. Three Ju-52's might be required to tow it.

## c. The X2A Heavy Glider

The heavy German glider X2A has been reported as capable of carrying 60 men with full equipment, or 40 men and two 37-mm guns, or 20 men and two 77-mm guns. Designed to be pulled by one Ju-52, the heaviest of this type is reputed to be equipped with auxiliary 8-cylinder motors.

# 24. TUG AND GLIDER PERFORMANCES

The tabulation in figure 5 is consolidated from all available sources. The calculations apply to still-air conditions, and vary by any change in those conditions, no allowance being made for evasive action, navigation errors, headwinds, etc. A reduction of radius of action or range required would, for instance, permit a corresponding increase of load to be taken by the towing plane.

The gliding distance for the DFS-230 glider has been calculated on the ratio of 1 to 16 (or even more): that is, for every foot of height at launching, the glider can theoretically cover 16 feet measured horizontally. In the attack on Crete it is reported that gliders were released at an altitude of 5,000 feet. This altitude, under normal conditions and with the loaded DFS-230 glider, would permit a gliding range of about 8 to 10 miles. However, all estimates as to gliding ranges are very uncertain, and subject to revision.

| | Take-off distance (ft) | Initial climb (ft per min) | Total range* | Mean speed with glider (in mph) and altitude (in ft) |
|---|---|---|---|---|
| Ju-52—fuel, 530 gals plus 1-ton payload. 1 Glider DFS-230 | ----- | ----- | 850 | 100/5,000 |
| Ju-52—fuel, 530 gals: | | | | |
|    1 Glider DFS-230 | 1,110 | ----- | 780 | 110/5,000 |
|    3 Gliders DFS-230 | 1,410 | 750 | 600 | 100/5,000 |
| Ju-52—fuel, 1,060 gals: | | | | |
|    1 Glider DFS-230 | 1,320 | 950 | 1,600 | 110/5,000 |
|    3 Gliders DFS-230 | 1,710 | 660 | 1,270 | 110/5,000 |
| 2 Ju-52—fuel, 1,060 gals each. 1 Glider Merseburg | 2,700 | 350 | 1,000 | 110/ |
| 3 Ju-52—fuel, 1,060 gals each. 1 Glider Go-242 | 2,610 | 340 | 990 | 110/5,000 |
| 1 Ju-52—fuel, 530 gals. 1 Glider Go-242 | 2,160 | 380 | 468 | 110/5,000 |
| Me-109—fuel, 154 gals. 1 Glider DFS-230 | 2,760 | 900 | 500 | 140/10,000 |
| Me-110—fuel, 280 gals. 1 Glider DFS-230 | 2,310 | 980 | 520 | 140/10,000 |
| Me-110—fuel (auxiliary tanks), 530 gals. 1 Glider | ----- | ----- | 760 | 210/ |

*Figure 5. Table of tug and glider performances (estimated)*

*\*Total range, the plane towing the glider all the way and not returning to base. A rough formula for calculating the plane's radius of action is the following: Range divided by 2 x .80 = Radius of action.*

## 25. THE DROPPING OF PARACHUTISTS FROM GLIDERS

It has often been reported that in training, men jump by parachute from gliders. Some observers reported that this method was used in Crete, but the reports are unconfirmed. It is certain that glider-borne troops do not normally wear parachutes (in Crete they had life jackets), and are technically not parachute troops but air-landing troops. Moreover, the DFS-230 is most unsuitable for the dropping of parachute troops.

## 26. SUCCESS AND WEAKNESS OF GLIDERS

The enemy was apparently satisfied with the success of the glider both in Belgium and in the Mediterranean. In Crete, however, it was found that the gliders were vulnerable if they came low near Allied troops. Their flight was very slow, and the crews could be killed before landing; hits in the forward part resulted in crashes, the pilot being killed or the reserve ammunition exploded. Where the ground was rocky, gliders were badly smashed on landing, and the crews and their equipment severely damaged. Some further disasters were due to mistakes by pilots; tow ropes snapped, owing, for instance, to the towing aircraft's making too short a turn, and gliders were released prematurely. This last mistake cost the lives of Major General Sussmann and his staff. In 1941-2, the construction of German gliders and the training of glider pilots was increased, and gliders were extensively employed for conveying material to North Africa. Their use is not restricted by any lack of air bases, for standard types of tow-planes like the Ju-52 do not require especially long runways. The latest gliders have been seen on some German airdromes which not only are small but which have no runways at all.

# GERMAN AIR-BORNE TRANSPORT

## 27. XIth AIR-BORNE CORPS

A German air-borne corps was first heard of early in 1941. This was the XIth Air-Borne Corps (called by the British, XI Air Corps), which contained the 7th Air-Borne Division and the 1st Assault Regiment. The XIth Air-Borne Corps is divided into two main parts: an air-transport organization and an air-transported part. The connections between the two are flexible in the sense that transport for any one unit of troops may be variously provided by different parts of the transport organization. (See fig. 6.)

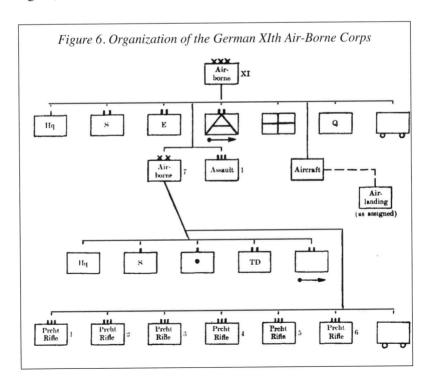

*Figure 6. Organization of the German XIth Air-Borne Corps*

## 28. GAF AIR-BORNE TROOPS AND ARMY AIR-LANDING TROOPS

In Holland and in Crete the German Air Force parachute troops were supported by army air-landing troops. It is believed that in any considerable undertaking the XIth Air-Borne Corps would be supported by army air-landing troops. Any ground troops can be pressed into such service, but, preferably, air-landing troops are taken from among the best infantry and mountain regiments, if possible only from combat regiments. Troops may be loaded into transport planes or even into gliders without having been previously trained in emplaning and deplaning. The Germans are quite prepared to do this on a mass basis.

## 29. THE IMPORTANCE OF NATIONAL AIR POWER

The size and qualities of a nation's air forces very directly influence its readiness for air-borne operations. Almost every kind of aircraft may conceivably be useful to insure the success of a well-planned undertaking. Troop-carrying and glider-towing planes, absolutely essential for mass air-borne transport, are the types to be emphasized below.

## 30. THE GERMAN TRANSPORT PLANE JU-52

The all-metal Ju-52 is the backbone of German airborne strength. So important is the Ju-52 that some observers have tended to believe that the Ju-52 was the basic factor in the makeup of the German system of airborne units. The German Army probably adopted the Ju-52 for air transport because there were so many of this type on hand at the beginning of the war, because so many supercharged engines were available, and because so many pilots had been trained on this type. Jigs and manufacturing facilities were already set up, and, though obsolescent, the Ju-52 had most of the following characteristics, which had been set up for a suggested new plane in this category: (1) Ability to operate in small or temporary fields with heavy

loads,

(2) Cheapness of construction,

(3) Simplicity and ruggedness of construction,

(4) Simplicity in operation,

(5) Easy field maintenance,

(6) Ability to fly with one engine out of commission.

(7) Ability to withstand crash landings with reasonable safety to occupants,

(8) Ability to tow gliders at low speed

(9) Dependability,

(10) Load-carrying capacity at sacrifice of speed.

## 31. THE GERMAN TRANSPORT PLANE JU-90

Another German transport type, the Ju-90, is also well adapted for the transport of troops and supplies, and especially adapted for transport of heavy and bulky articles. However, this type is so valuable that it is rarely risked in forward areas, or on airdromes that the Germans do not firmly control. In March 1942, the Germans by one estimate were not thought to have more than 40 Ju-90's.

*The high level of casualties suffered by the Fallschirmjäger in Crete led to the cancellation of all future large scale operations.*

## 32. THE PRINCIPAL ADVANTAGE OF THE JU-52 AND THE JU-90

The manner in which loads are to be packed and unpacked for an air-borne operation is fully as important as the weight to be carried by available aircraft. Some items, though not too heavy, may be too bulky to be loaded; again, if the plane is to carry bicycles or passengers, obviously it may not carry its maximum tonnage. Speed in deplaning is so essential in most air-borne operations that it is rather unusual to load a Ju-52 to anything like its weight-carrying capacity. It has been said that the outstanding advantage of the Ju-52 and the Ju-90 is that their trapdoors can be opened almost as wide as the aircraft on either the top or the bottom of the fuselage.

## 33. COMPARISON OF THE JU-52 WITH THE JU-90

The tabulation in figure 7 shows how the Ju-52 and the Ju-90 compare in a number of important particulars. The Ju-90 has two types of engines, either radial or liquid-cooled. Performances shown in the right-hand column are for the Ju-90 with liquid-cooled engines.

## 34. RANGE AND LOAD OF GERMAN TRANSPORT AIRCRAFT

The estimated range and useful load of several types of German transport aircraft are shown in the following table, loads and ranges being variable:*

| Transport Type | Cargo Weight | Maximum Range |
|---|---|---|
| Ju-52 (some on pontons) | 3,000 lbs | 1,070 mi |
| Ju-52 | 5,000 lbs | 780 mi |
| Ju-52 | 7,500 lbs | 250 mi |
| Ju-86 | 5,000 lbs | 930 mi |
| Ju-90 | 15,000 lbs | 1,300 mi |
| FW-200 | 13,700 lbs | 1,275 mi |
| FW-200 | 10,000 lbs | 770 mi |

*Range depends partly on speed.

| | Ju-52 | | | Ju-90 | |
|---|---|---|---|---|---|
| **Description** | 3-engined low-wing metal monoplane | | | 4-engined low-wing all-metal monoplane | |
| **Wing span** | 96 ft | | | 115 ft | |
| **Wing area** | 1,190 ft | | | 1,980 ft | |
| **Length** | 62 ft | | | 85 ft | |
| **Height** | 15 ft | | | 21 ft | |
| **Armament** | One 7.9-mm MG, forward | | | One 7.9-mm MG, forward fuselage | |
| | One 7.9-mm MG, ventral | | | One 7.9-mm MG, tail | |
| | Two 7.9-mm MG, lateral | | | One 13-mm MG, dorsal | |
| | One 7.9-mm MG, forward | | | | |
| **Weight:** | Empty (including radio): | | | Empty with equipment, 36,200 lbs | |
| | Civilian passenger type, 13,255 lbs | | | Normal all up weight, 51,000 lbs | |
| | Military passenger type, 12,720 lbs | | | Overload weight, 54,000 lbs | |
| | Freight aircraft, 12,420 lbs | | | Disposable load at maximum overload, 29,800 lbs | |
| | Normal loaded weight, 20,300 lbs | | | | |
| | Overload weight, 23,100 lbs | | | | |
| **Performance:** | Maximum speed, 180 mph at 5,500 ft | | | Maximum speed, 218 mph at 3,500 ft | |
| | (165 at sea level) | | | Maximum speed, 260 mph at 15,000 ft | |
| | Cruising speed at 70%, 180 mph | | | Cruising speed, 230 mph | |
| | (132 at sea level) | | | Cruising speed at 5,000 ft, 177 mph | |
| | Landing speed at normal weight, 62 mph | | | | |
| | Ceiling 20,000 ft | | | Ceiling: 19,000 ft | |
| **Typical loads and performances** | | | | | |
| *Useful load* | 3,000 lbs | 5,000 lbs | 7,500 lbs | 22,000 lbs | 10,000 lbs |
| *Range (mi)* | 1,070-830 | 780-600 | 250-190 | 800 | 2,200 |
| *Speed (mph)* | 110-140 | 120-150 | 120-150 | 230 | 230 |
| *Bomb capacity* | Maximum 5,000 lbs | | | Normal 4,400 lbs | |

*Figure 7. Table comparing the Ju-52 and the Ju-90*

51

*A soldier of 3rd Division guards two German paratroopers captured at Caen, 11 July 1944.*

# 35. AIR TRANSPORT ORGANIZATION

Transport planes are generally organized in a wing (Geschwader) of 4 groups (Gruppen), each group having 4 squadrons (Staffeln) of 12 planes each plus a headquarters squadron, as further explained below. With each Ju-52 carrying approximately 10 men fully equipped one of these wings will transport a parachute regiment with all its equipment.

It is reported that such Z.B.V. transport units (Zur Besonderen Verwendung, for special employment) were used on the Russian Front in 1942 for bringing up supplies of fuel and ammunition and, probably, delivering provisions to troops in forward areas and returning to their bases with wounded. The more active areas for air transport continue to be Northern France, Belgium, Holland, Northern Germany, and the Russian Front. There has been also, of course, trans-Mediterranean traffic to and from Libya.

## 36. TRANSPORT OF A GERMAN AIR-BORNE DIVISION

It has been mentioned above that no long training period is necessary to prepare a normal German division for use in an air-infantry operation. The preparation is more a problem of organization than one of training. The German 22d Infantry Regiment was reorganized as an Air-Borne Infantry Division in 1940, and, as such, it took part in the campaign in Holland. It should be noted that this division is particularly strong in staff organization, which, of course, is desirable for supervision and to compensate for probable loss among the staff during transport by air and during early ground action. The approximate power of this division was estimated in late 1940 as follows:

- Officers: 241
- Noncommissioned officers: 1,105
- Enlisted men: 5,334
- Mountain cannon, 75-mm: 24
- Antitank cannon, 37-mm: 30
- Heavy machine guns: 60
- Light machine guns: 125
- Antiaircraft guns, 20-mm: 16
- Light infantry cannon: 3
- Light grenade throwers: 54
- Heavy grenade throwers: 36
- Antitank rifles (Panzerbüchsen): 112
- Machine pistols: 375
- Rifles: 4,371

Any discrepancy between heavy machine guns and antitank weapons shown in the above tabulation and those listed in an organization chart may be due to extra weapons carried in reserve. On the way to combat, troops of this division had in their packs 2 days' rations in addition to the "iron" ration. No field kitchens were carried. It was intended to use the kitchens in hotels and inns, and, after the first 3 days, to requisition food and all vehicles from the civil population, if necessary.

## a. Operational Experience in Holland

A loading unit (Ladeeinheit) is a load of men and equipment or both together, sufficient for one Ju-52. In the operation at The Hague, the total number of loading units was not less than 866, and the number of men in the "division" transported has been calculated as 7,400. This works out at between 8 and 9 men (with proportional share of divisional equipment) per Ju-52. Of the planes transporting the divisional staff, none carried more than 9 men. Infantry traveled at 12 or even 14 men per plane; engineers at about 10 per plane; motorcycle units, with solo machines, at 6 or 7 per plane. A light infantry gun probably was accompanied by about 6 men in the same plane, while probably 2 more planes would carry the ammunition and additional personnel.

## b. Operational Experience in the Conquest of Crete

For the attack on Crete, the Germans are thought to have carried fewer men and more equipment per Ju-52. The ordinary infantry battalion may have traveled at only about 10 men, with equipment, per Ju-52. The number of aircraft which the Germans used in the operation is conservatively estimated at nearly 800 bombers and fighters, 500 transport planes, and 75 gliders. In any case it is not thought that more than 650 Ju-52's were employed. To get something like 35,000 men to Crete in a period of 10 days, it is estimated that each Ju-52 must have made on the average about 6 sorties.

# 37. TRANSPORT OF AIR-LANDING TROOPS BY JU-52's

The following table gives the approximate number of loading units required to transport various organizations with their organizational equipment. The calculations take into account a reduction to combat strength for air transport, but composition and armament are obviously subject to further variation depending upon special circumstances:

| | Appropriate Loading Units (1 per each Ju-52) |
|---|---|
| Inf Rifle Co | 12 |
| Inf Hv Wpns Co | 21 |
| Inf Bn Hq | 3 |
| Inf Regtl Hq and Com Det | 5 |
| Arty Btry (with 75-mm Mtn guns only) | 16 |
| Arty Bn Hq (with 75-mm Mtn guns only) | 6 |
| Arty Regtl Hq and Com Det (with 75-mm Mtn guns only) | 18 |
| AA MG Co | 12 |
| AT Co | 14 |
| Div Med Co | 14 |
| Div Sup Co | 14 |
| Inf Div Hq | 12 |

# 38. TRANSPORTATION OF GERMAN PARACHUTE UNITS

German parachute units and equipment are specially adapted to fit into the Ju-52 system of transportation. In both Crete and Holland it has been demonstrated that the following loading practices are customary:

### a. Transportation of a Parachute Company

One company of parachute troops is transported by one squadron (Staffel) of Ju-52's (12 aircraft). In the case of the parachute rifle company, every Ju-52 carries 12 men and 4 arms containers. The precise loading units for the parachute heavy weapons company are not known. Each Ju-52 takes rather more than one section, and each flight (Kette) of three aircraft rather less than one platoon. There seems to be no rigorous attempt to fly by platoon,

*Fallschirmjäger in preparation for Operation Marita.*

though aircraft must fly in the order planned, and land their men on the right spots with the right arms containers. The real working unit is the company.

## b. Light Relative Load

The weight of the load carried by each Ju-52 in a squadron lifting a parachute rifle company is about 4,000 pounds, including the plane's own crew of three men. Considerations of bulk and of speed in leaving the plane dictate this relatively light load, which allows 100 pounds of equipment per man:

- 15 men with clothes and equipment on person: 2,400 lbs
- 4 arms containers: 1,200 lbs
- 19 parachutes: 450 lbs
- Total load lifted by each Ju-52: 4,050 lbs

## c. Transportation of a Parachute Battalion

One parachute rifle battalion is transported by one group (Gruppe) of Ju-52's (53 aircraft). The four companies are transported by the four squadrons of the group; and the battalion headquarters with its communication section is transported by the headquarters squadron (Stabsstaffel) of five aircraft.

### d. Transportation of a Parachute Regiment

One parachute regiment is transported by one wing (Geschwader) of Ju-52's (220 aircraft). The three parachute battalions are transported by three of the groups in the wing; and the "fourth battalion," or regimental headquarters with regimental troops, is transported by the fourth group.

### e. Transportation of a Parachute Division

One parachute division could be carried by four wings of Ju-52's (880 aircraft). The three parachute regiments would be carried by three wings, and divisional headquarters with divisional troops (signal company, artillery battery, machine-gun battalion, and antitank battalion) by the fourth wing. But up to the spring of 1942 no division had yet been transported at a single lift.

### f. Loading of Non-Divisional Units

Not much is known of the loading of non-divisional parachute units (engineer battalion, anti-aircraft machine-gun battalion, and medical unit). It seems probable that each would be carried by one group of Ju-52's, in the proportion of one company to one squadron.

## 39. COMMUNICATIONS IN AIR-BORNE OPERATIONS

The theory of air-borne attack presupposes assault upon a hostile area under conditions wherein the only link with the higher command is through means of communication carried with the attacking troops or improvised by them. Portable radio sets constitute the basic means of establishing contact with other units, with headquarters, and with the friendly aircraft operating in the area. Because of the likelihood of heavy casualties during the early phases of the attack, assault units are provided with about twice the amount of radio equipment ordinarily assigned to ground combat units of the same size. A parachute rifle battalion appears to be equipped with two radio subsections for battalion-to-regiment communication, and eight very high-frequency radio subsections for point-to-point communication on the general company-to-company circuit.

## a. Types of Radios

German air-borne attack troops, during the operations at Crete, were equipped with several types of radios, but two types were most extensively used. The pack "b.1," which was carried in three parts, weighed about 120 pounds all told. Operating on a frequency of 3,000 to 5,000 kilocycles, the "b.1" transmitter had a range of from 10 to 15 miles. The pack "d.2" (very high frequency) weighed about 40 pounds and had a range of 7 1/2 to 10 miles. This model operated on 33,800 to 38,000 kilocycles. Both of these sets, being very light, are well suited for use by air-borne units.

## b. Visual Communication

Ground-to-air visual communication is accomplished by a variety of means: by flags, by colored smoke signals, and by panels. During the Crete operations, swastika flags were used to denote German troops. White or yellow ground panels of cloth were used to indicate front lines. Headquarters positions were indicated by panels in the form of a cross, and spots where supplies were to be dropped by two "X's", side by side. Direction of resistance was indicated by inverted "V's" with the point in the direction of the resistance. Various other panel designs were similarly employed to convey prearranged messages. Green smoke signals were used to attract the attention of aircraft where supplies were wanted. Red smoke signals are also believed to have been used, to indicate enemy defended positions. In Crete some British learned the German panel calls and used them to send for reinforcements (whom they shot), for food (which they gladly ate), and for other supplies.

*The ever present danger of attack by Allied fighter bombers mandated that all vehicles were disguised to the fullest possible extent.*

# CONCLUSIONS: ENEMY AIR-BORNE TACTICS

Although U.S. troops at Pearl Harbor and since have undergone numerous air attacks, up to autumn 1942 they have experienced no air-borne assaults. But because all of the Axis enemies, notably the arch-teacher Germany and the arch-pupil Japan, are capable of planning such assaults, it is worthwhile to consider the tactical lessons learned by the British from the classic Battle of Crete. Their conclusions have been summed up in very nearly the following words, which are changed mainly to allow for several differences in nomenclature.

## 40. DISTANCE FROM DEPARTURE AIRDROMES

It is remarkable that the distance from departure airdromes to the scene of operations in Crete was approximately the same as it was previously in the attack on Holland, namely about 200 miles. If the departure airdromes are too near to the objective, they may be discovered in time (the concentrations of transport planes being conspicuous), and the advantages of surprise will be forfeited, even if the force is not, as is likely to happen, shot up before it starts. On the other hand, there are many reasons why the distance from rear headquarters to objectives must not be very great:

(1) If fighter support is to be provided, the distance must be kept within the radius of action of that type of aircraft.

(2) Over longer distances, more aircraft are needed to keep up ferrying.

(3) Over longer distances, decisions made at the rear take progressively longer to affect the action.

(4) Troops going into action should not be kept seated in aircraft too long.

(5) The attack itself cannot begin at dawn, unless the take-off is made by night; there is, however, everything to be said for attacking early in the day, and therefore for taking off at dawn and not spending too long on the journey. A journey of even 200 miles takes, with gliders, 2 hours (actually, it took the gliders 3 hours to get from Tanagra to Canea).

(6) In general, the operation becomes progressively more difficult for pilots over longer distances.

One must not forget that it is difficult to state definitely any particular limitation on aircraft that will hold good for an indefinite period. Overloading has been systematically practiced for years for the purpose of attaining a certain objective. Refueling from the air was regularly practiced in British transoceanic passenger demonstrations some years ago. Extra tanks added to the Me-109 made possible a 310-mile radius (620-mile range), and the immediate use of belly tanks by the Japanese raised the normal range of their fighters from approximately 800 to 1,200 miles. Recent reports have stated that U.S. parachute troops have been flown 1,500 miles to combat in North Africa.

# 41. PRELIMINARY BOMBING AND MACHINE-GUNNING

The Germans are likely to subject the areas where descents by air-borne troops are intended to take place to a short but intensive preliminary dive-bombing and machine-gunning attack against such objectives as anti-aircraft guns, airdrome defenses, and troop positions. Accompanying fighter support will also be used where resistance by Allied fighters is anticipated. In Crete, though Allied troops had no fighter cover, casualties directly attributable to dive-bombing attacks were comparatively few when troops were dispersed and in foxholes (slit trenches),

*A Fallschirmjäger machine gun team in Italy during 1943.*

although these attacks greatly hampered movement of the defending forces by day. This bombing will cease in the areas selected for descents as soon as the airborne troops start to arrive, but is likely to be continued all around the objective. At Malemé the dust of the air bombardment hid from view the first landings, which were made by gliders.

## 42. PROSPECTIVE PATTERN FOR AIR-BORNE ATTACK

The air bombardment is likely to be followed by an air-borne attack, which may take the following form:

a. A preliminary wave of shock troops (probably at least in part glider-borne) to achieve surprise with the task of neutralizing anti-aircraft and other defenses and dislocating communications.

b. Following immediately on this, descents of parachute troops with the task of seizing a landing ground; these descents may be at several points, 15 to 20 miles apart.

c. Later, possibly by several hours, strong reinforcements of parachute troops followed or accompanied by troops in transport aircraft in those areas where the first wave has been successful. Air-landing troops, theoretically, arrive as soon as a landing ground is prepared, but in case of necessity may arrive even earlier.

## 43. TACTICS OF SHOCK TROOPS

Normally the shock troops will work by companies. They will be instructed to get in touch with neighboring units, probably battalions or regiments, as soon as possible. After accomplishing their initial task, they will be instructed to join up with, and take orders from the higher units which have subsequently descended. For this, radio communication will be essential. It should be noticed that glider-borne troops, though technically "air-landing" troops, operate in close conjunction with parachute troops. Having their arms with them, and not being dispersed, they are able to go into action even more quickly than parachute troops.

## 44. DISRUPTION OF COMMUNICATIONS

Great importance is attached to the dislocation of communications. In any undefended area handfuls of the enemy landed stealthily from the air may be expected to exert surprise and dismay out of all proportion to their numbers by destroying telephone or telegraph installations, seizing radio stations, and interfering with the ordinary channels of communication. Such a dislocation may be undertaken as a temporary diversion or other special operation, or as the preliminary to a larger airborne attack.

## 45. GROUND ASSEMBLY OF AIR-BORNE TROOPS

Main bodies of parachute troops will be instructed to attack their objectives (an airdrome, town, or military position) as a coordinated unit or force. Tactics, of course, may be expected to vary, depending upon the objective. Before an attack of any importance is launched, companies will get into contact with battalions, and battalions with regiments. Companies may descend some distance apart (say half a mile to a mile and a half), but they will try so to land that they can operate as a normal infantry unit. To produce the requisite coordination, radio communication will be essential from the moment the descent is complete. The dropping zone of one main attacking body may be as much as 24 square miles; in Crete the density at which parachute troops were dropped on the first day was from 400 to 500 (about 1 battalion) per square mile.

## 46. VULNERABILITY OF PARACHUTISTS

The first task of parachute troops is to collect and assemble weapons and munitions dropped separately by parachute, for the men are comparatively lightly armed for the drop. (While they are getting out of their harness and collecting arms and equipment from containers, parachutists are by no means defenseless, for they have their carbines, pistols, and grenades). In Crete, however, those who dropped in areas occupied by Allied troops suffered such heavy casualties that their inclination was to hide and take no active part in proceedings for several hours. Experience showed that parachute troops were most vulnerable for the few minutes after they had landed, but if they were given time to assemble into organized bodies, they recovered their morale. The enemy has learned the lesson that it is disastrous to drop parachute troops actually among the defending troops. Also, in the future the enemy will probably make every effort to drop even heavy equipment complete and ready for action, if possible without containers.

## 47. THE DROPPING ZONE FOR PARACHUTISTS

Parachute troops are therefore likely to be dropped in depth around any airdromes or areas selected for attack, instead of being concentrated on the site itself.3 After carrying out short preliminary tasks, they will then form up for coordinated attack. The use of smoke laid by aircraft in the actual dropping zone of

*A Fallschirmjäger anti-tank crew on the Italian front.*

parachute troops is considered unlikely. Parachute troops are, however, well equipped to make tactical use of smoke on the ground. They also may carry a few tear-gas bombs.

(Parachute troops can be landed in most but not all types of country. The ideal is to have an area of unobstructed, flat, soft ground, some 1,000 by 600 yards, which constitutes a zone on which some 50 troops can be put down simultaneously every 5 minutes with comparative safety and lack of confusion. Hedges and occasional trees really constitute no obstruction, but rocky or obstructed grounds, or high winds (over 30 miles per hour) will normally cause injuries.)

## 48. REINFORCEMENT OF SUCCESS

Like all German operations, an Axis air-borne attack will be based on and is particularly suited to the principle of reinforcing success. The initial plan will be only a short-term one, the later stages depending entirely on reports of initial successes being received at directing headquarters. Plans will be bold and probably not expected to succeed in all cases.

## 49. NECESSITY FOR EARLY REINFORCEMENT

Although it is known that in Crete the air-landing troops did not

*Fallschirmjäger deployed in shell holes created by heavy artillery on the russian front.*

arrive in strength until the day following the initial parachute attack, it is thought that the Germans would, in face of air fighter defenses, mobile reserves, and organized land defenses, be compelled to reinforce their parachute troops at the earliest moment. Command will be taken over by commanders of army troops, who will have had a large share in framing the comprehensive plan of attack.

## 50. LACK OF MOBILITY OF GROUNDED AIR-BORNE TROOPS

It is not clear how light tanks, if brought, would be employed. The great handicap of all air-borne troops is their lack of mobility; once they are on the ground, they are heavily laden with weapons and equipment. They might thus be quite unable, at least in the early stages, to follow up tank advances. In any case, German opinion is increasingly unfavorable to the vulnerable light tank; and for attacks on strong posts, such as concrete pillboxes, it favors the use of antitank weapons and of infantry shock troops, with explosives. The plan seems to be, rather, to bring as much motor transport as possible, especially tractors, to make possible the movement of reasonably heavy weapons, especially infantry and AT guns. After seizing the objective, by dint of surprise and shock-infantry tactics, the troops will then be equipped to meet counter-attacks.

## 51. DETERRENT EFFECT OF DARKNESS

No air-borne operations have yet been carried out by night. A descent on a moonlit night is considered possible, but the difficulty with which detachments would be confronted in accurately determining their position is likely to cause them to defer any attack until dawn. Tactics would then be similar to those following a daylight descent; but surprise would have been forfeited. A descent on a very dark night is unlikely.

## 52. GROUND-TO-AIR VISUAL SIGNALLING

Direct radio communication between troops in action and supporting aircraft is less to be anticipated than ground-to-air visual signaling. Supplies (of which enough for a few days only are taken initially) will be demanded by means of flags, panels, and perhaps flares. Bogus panels and flags would effectively confuse pilots, as was successfully done in Crete. Air support will be demanded by radio only indirectly, by way of rear headquarters and the headquarters of the supporting air unit.

## 53. RADIO COMMUNICATION

Air-borne troops will depend more than ordinary infantry on the use of radio, at least until they have overcome any immediate opposition and have become a coordinated force. Thereafter, they will act as ordinary infantry and will not be so entirely dependent on radio communication, except for traffic with their rear headquarters. In the early stages of an operation, much depends on reports being received at rear headquarters from reconnaissance aircraft and forward units; in the later stages, the key points are the "flying radio stations" and the radio sets at headquarters of forward groups. It should be possible to jam some of this traffic with good results.

# APPENDIX A

## AN INTIMATE REPORT ON A FORMER MEMBER OF THE GERMAN 5th PARACHUTE REGIMENT

### 1. CIVILIAN BACKGROUND

XY was born September 27, 1922, at Merlebach (Moselle). He was brought up at Ludweiler (Saar), where his father was employed during the French occupation that followed World War I. After 3 years of primary schooling at Ludweiler he attended High School at Teltow, south of Berlin; next, the Technical University at Frankenhausen (Thuringia); and finally the Mine Specialist School at Saarbrücken. In August 1939, on the eve of World War II, he was evacuated with his parents to Thuringia. From that time on he attended the Mining School at Freiberg (Saxony). Repatriated to Saarbrücken, he resumed his studies at the Mining Specialist School of that city in August 1940.

### 2. MILITARY ENLISTMENT

On December 17, 1940, his recruiting classification gave the eighteen-year-old-youth the choice either of volunteering immediately for the German Air Force without labor service or of joining the infantry with labor service in April 1941.

### 3. INCORPORATION INTO THE 1ST PARACHUTE REPLACEMENT REGIMENT (STENDAL)

XY chose the Air Force and asked to serve as a parachutist. He was ordered to report on December 18, 1940, at the 1st Parachute Replacement Regiment at Stendal (Aitmark). At that time, all the parachutist replacement units and all the parachutist schools were under the command of Colonel Ramcke, who reportedly

*A dramatic panorama as German paratroopers land in Crete, May 1941.*

was the oldest parachutist of the army. Ramcke later distinguished himself during the campaign of Crete, after which he was promoted to General Major (Brigadier General) and decorated with the Knight's Cross. As soon as XY arrived at the 1st Parachute Replacement Regiment, he was asked whether he would like to become an officer. Several of his comrades accepted the offer and were sent immediately in the grade of cadet captain (Fahnenjunker) to the school at Fassberg (Lüneburger Heide). On declining this offer, XY was sent to the 4th Battalion of the 1st Parachute Replacement Regiment, where he remained 4 days and received the first general notions about the Army. During these 4 days also he was supposed to assimilate the whole School of the Soldier. Discipline was extremely severe.

## 4. TRANSFER TO THE 3d BATTALION OF THE 1st PARACHUTE REPLACEMENT REGIMENT AT HELMSTETT, THEN TO FASSBURG

From Stendal, XY was transferred to the 3d Battalion, 1st Parachute Replacement Regiment, at Helmstett. After a few days this battalion was moved to Fassburg, where the largest flying school of the German Air Force was then located and where a parachute instruction center was being developed. As soon as he arrived at Fassburg, XY was assigned to the regiment's 10th Company, which was composed of 4 platoons of 36 men each. The two first platoons had 6 heavy mortars apiece. The instruction in this company lasted until the end of January 1941, that is, about a month. It consisted of instruction in heavy weapons (heavy machine guns and heavy mortars), individual combat, and section combat.

## 5. STAY AT THE PARACHUTE-JUMPING SCHOOL AT WITTSTOCK

After repeated medical examinations which involved chiefly the nerves, heart, lungs, feet, and muscles, XY was sent at the beginning of February 1941 to the Parachute-Jumping School of Wittstock on the Dosse. His training at this school lasted 26 days. For the first 12 days, 2 hours per day were devoted to technical instruction in the parachute and its folding. The other hours were given over to rigorous athletic training, especially in jiu-jitsu, and in trapeze and rope work. The daily program left the students completely worn out by evening. The 13th and 14th days were devoted exclusively to practical exercises in folding the parachute. The 15th to the 26th days, inclusive, were devoted to parachute-jumping exercises.

## 6. PARACHUTE-JUMPING EXERCISES

The first jump was made from an altitude of 725 feet, one man jumping at a time, that is, each time the plane passed the field chosen. The second and third jumps were from an altitude of 600 feet, 6 men jumping in rapid succession every time the plane flew over the field. The fifth, sixth, and seventh jumps were made from altitudes varying from 500 to 360 feet. On each of these jumps, 12 men, comprising a section, had to jump in rapid succession. After the 6th jump, the students were told that during combat, if a rapid-firing and well-adjusted AA gun rendered it necessary, the parachutists would perhaps be dropped from altitudes of 270 to 225 feet only; but the men were warned that in such cases their parachutes might not open in time fully to check the fall and avoid a violent landing on the ground.

## 7. REMARKS ON THESE TRAINING JUMPS

For these jumps, the only parachutes used were the RZ16. The airplanes used were Ju-52's. To be considered fit for combat with his branch, a parachutist must have made six jumps in a training school.

## 8. FURTHER STAY AT THE 1ST PARACHUTE REGIMENT AT STENDAL

From February 28 to March 5, 1941, XY followed a course of special instruction on the flame-thrower, the machine pistol, and the combat pistol. During these 6 days, the instruction continued almost without interruption; the students had the privilege of sleeping only 3 hours out of each 24.

## 9. STAY AT THE 1ST BATTALION OF THE 1ST PARACHUTE ASSAULT REGIMENT

On March 8, 1941, XY was assigned to the 1st Battalion of the 1st Parachute Assault Regiment at Hildesheim (Hanover). The 1st Parachute Assault Regiment was the first created (and remained the only one subsequently) of a series of parachutist assault regiments which were to contain the pick of the elite. This regiment was commanded by Brigadier General Meindl. The 1st Battalion, Hildesheim, was commanded by an officer already well known as the victor of Eben Emael and of the Albert Canal, Major Koch, who had been decorated with the Ritterkreuz. The 2d Battalion was at Goslar and the 3d at Halberstadt.

## 10. TRAINING IN THE USE OF FOREIGN WEAPONS

In this regiment, discipline was severe, training was intensive, and technical instruction was decidedly advanced. Much insistence was paid to the various French, English, Czech, and Italian weapons. During the period March 10 to April 25, 1941, the regiment made stays at the Sennelager Camp and at the Bergen Camp.

## 11. DEPARTURE FOR A SECRET DESTINATION

On April 26, 1941, the 1st Parachute Assault Regiment was given new uniforms and all its weapons were packed in weapon containers. On April 29, 1941, the regiment proceeded in trucks from its various barracks for a destination known only to the superior officers. XY remembers having passed through Leipzig, Dresden, Prague, Vienna, Budapest, and Bucharest to the Bulgarian frontier. Here the parachutists stopped for a few days, and they were told that the regiment would go into action at Megara in Greece on the Corinth Isthmus.

## 12. ACCIDENT AT THERMOPYLAE

At historic Thermopylae Pass in northern Greece, the truck on which XY was travelling overturned in the congestion and some of his comrades were killed. XY, seriously wounded, was transported in an airplane to Salonica and later to Athens. Consequently, he took no part in the Crete campaign.

## 13. RETURN FROM GREECE TO GERMANY

On July 10, when XY rejoined the 1st Parachute Assault Regiment at Megara, he found that the regiment had suffered a minimum of 60 Percent in casualties, three-fourths of whom had been killed outright. On July 20, the regiment left Megara to return to its garrison town in Germany, where the survivors were welcomed as heroes. The men were then given new uniforms and 27-day furloughs.

## 14. REORGANIZATION OF THE REGIMENT

At the end of August 1941, the regiment was brought up to strength in a provisional manner by elements from the infantry, so that it had an average of only 40 percent of trained parachutists. During the whole month of September 1941, the regiment was put through a very stiff program of training, consisting of advanced infantry and engineer training. At the end of September 1941, the 2d Battalion of Goslar was broken up and divided between the 1st and 3d (garrisoned at Hildesheim and Halberstadt), which thus obtained a proportion of 60 percent of trained parachutists. It should be mentioned that the trained parachutists (those having at least six jumps in a school) received a parachutist's pay, which meant an increase of 60 marks per month.

## 15. EMPLOYMENT OF THE REGIMENT AGAINST THE RUSSIANS

From the month of September, it was rumored in the regiment that its parachutists were going to be employed in Russia as infantry and engineers. As a matter of fact, from the beginning of October 1941, the battalions (not only of this regiment but of ordinary parachute regiments) left one after another for the region of Leningrad. XY got out of this campaign because he was ordered to take a course in telegraphy which lasted 4 months. During the month of February 1942, the remnants of the 1st and 2d Battalions of the 1st Parachute Assault Regiment returned from Russia to their garrison town of Hildersheim and Halberstadt. They had lost about 65 to 70 percent in casualties, including many officers; among others, Major Stenzler, ex-commander of the 2d Battalion.

## 16. ASSIGNMENT TO THE 5TH PARACHUTE REGIMENT

XY at that time was away on a 20-day furlough. Upon arrival at his station, he learned that the 1st Parachute Assault Regiment had been broken up and that, with the remainder, the 5th Parachute Regiment was being formed. XY was assigned to the 2d Battalion of the 5th Parachute Regiment. The regiment was under the command of Lieutenant Colonel Koch, who had been wounded twice in the head during the Crete campaign and had been promoted for exceptional bravery before Leningrad.

*A Fallschirmjäger in mid-descent.*

## 17. INTENSIVE INFANTRY INSTRUCTIONS

After a month and a half of instruction at its station, especially in infantry tactics, the regiment made a stay of 1 month at the Grossborn Camp near Neustettin, where infantry instruction was continued, with emphasis on day and night foot marches of 20, 25, and even 30 miles, with complete infantry equipment.

## 18. DEPARTURE FOR FRANCE

On May 17, 1942, the 5th Parachute Regiment left the Grossborn Camp by rail for France, where it was to take part in the defense of the coast. It followed the itinerary, Stettin - Berlin - Aix-la-Chapelle - Holland - Belgium - Lille - Rouen - Coutances. The regimental staff, the 2d Battalion and the cannon and antitank companies remained garrisoned at Coutances. The 1st Battalion went to Coutainville, the 3d Battalion to Avranches. The latter battalion made the trip from Coutances to Avranches on foot from 0100 to 1200 on May 20, 1942. At Avranches they were quartered at Notre Dame Institute, which was found to be occupied by only a few priests.

## 19. INCIDENTS IN THE DEFENSE OF THE CHANNEL COAST AGAINST ALLIED INVASION

During the night of May 20 to 21, the 3d Battalion was alerted and continued on towards the west. But upon arrival of a counterorder toward morning, the battalion was given a 2-day rest, during which numerous reconnaissances of the coast were made for the purpose of determining what defensive fortification was to be carried out. As soon as the newcomers reached the Channel Coast, everybody lived under fear of an Allied debarkation, the more so since a few days before the arrival of the 3d Battalion of the 5th Parachute Regiment at Avranches, an English coup-de-main had succeeded in capturing in silence, on the coast right close to the city, a German guard of the strength of a combat section; the English commander had written on the guard's register: "Guard completely overpowered; we'll be back soon." The 3d Battalion was immediately obliged to furnish numerous guard detachments. Moreover, each company had to form a reinforced alert platoon (4 sections - about 45 men). Such platoons were formed into an alert company which was kept under arms 24 hours out of 24, well supplied with ammunition and explosives. For rapid transportation, the battalion requisitioned five large buses which were kept always in readiness for the alert company. The remaining men of the battalion were used to help construct field fortifications along the coast.

# APPENDIX B

## INTELLIGENCE INFORMATION ON THE GERMAN 5th PARACHUTE REGIMENT

### 1. COMPOSITION OF THE REGIMENT

On account of its composition, the 5th Parachute Regiment resembles an infantry regiment in every respect: it includes -

- Regimental staff,
- 3 identical battalions of 4 companies each,
- 1 infantry cannon company (13th),
- 1 AT Company (14th),
- 1 regimental engineer platoon of about 50 men.

### 2. THE ENGINEER PLATOON

Theoretically, the regiment should have an engineer company of the same strength and general structure as an ordinary company. This engineer company actually existed before and during the Cretan Campaign in the various parachutist regiments, and especially in the 1st Parachute Assault Regiment which gave birth to the 5th Parachute Regiment. Owing to the lack of manpower, this company was reduced to the size of a strong platoon.

### 3. ACTIVATION OF THE REGIMENT

The 5th Parachute Regiment was formed at the end of February or the beginning of March 1942 from the following elements:

a. About 750 men remaining from the 1st and 3d Battalions of the 1st Parachute Assault Regiment upon arrival from Russia, beginning February 1942. The 2d Battalion had been broken up subsequent to September 1941 to complete the two other battalions before their departure for Russia.)

b. About 90 men remaining from the 14th Company of the 1st Parachute Assault Regiment when it returned from Russia at the beginning of March 1942.

c. A total of 180 men in the stations of Halberstadt, Hildesheirn and Goslar-Heimstett, formed the "Rest-Kommandos" (rear party) of the 1st Parachute Regiment (during the stay of the latter in Russia).

d. The 13th Company of the 1st Parachute Assault Regiment, which had not been sent to Russia.

e. An increment of 160 men furnished by the 9th Company of the 1st Parachute Regiment of Dedelstorf.

f. About 100 men supplied by the 11th Company of the 1st Parachute Replacement Regiment.

g. About 1,400 men furnished by the 2d Battalion of the 1st Parachute Replacement Regiment at Weissewarte and the 4th Battalion of the 1st Parachute Replacement Regiment at Tangermunde.

## 4. REDUCTION OF EXCESS STRENGTH

In any case, when the general call took place at Grossborn during the first 10 days of May, it was found that the 5th Parachute Regiment had a total strength of 3,000 officers, NCO's, and men. This strength appears to have surpassed the actual authorized strength, since, when a verification took place in early June, there was found in the regiment an excess of 600 men, who were to be transferred before June 25 into an aviation unit stationed in the region of Bremen. (On this occasion the company commanders made a selection of their men and got rid of the worst.)

## 5. THE REGIMENTAL COMMANDER: LIEUTENANT COLONEL KOCH

Lieutenant Colonel Koch, a personal friend of Marshal Goering, is only 28 years old. He distinguished himself by the capture of Fort Eben Emael and by the crossing of the Albert Canal. As former commander of the 1st Battalion, 1st Parachute Assault Regiment, during the Cretan Campaign, he was twice wounded in the head by bullets. Promoted to a lieutenant-colonelcy near Leningrad, he came back from Russia on May 15, 1942, 2 days before the departure of the 5th Parachute Regiment for France.

## 6. DEGREE OF SPECIAL INSTRUCTION OF THE 5TH PARACHUTE REGIMENT

On June 18, 1942, the 5th Parachute Regiment was short of many trained parachutists. Only the following units contained trained parachutists exclusively: The Regimental Headquarters, the 2d Battalion, the cannon company, and the antitank company. These units had been at the Wittstock "jumping school" from April 15 to May 15, 1942, while the 5th Parachute Regiment was at Grossborn camp. The other units of the Regiment did not contain more than 20 to 25 percent of trained parachutists. About June 15, rumor had it that the 3d Battalion was to be sent to a "jumping school" functioning in the neighborhood of Paris.

## 7. SPECIFIC INFORMATION CONCERNING THE REGIMENT AS OF JUNE 1942:

a. The Regiment did not have its parachutes with it, these having been left at the former stations of Halberstadt, Hildesheim, and Goslar-Helmstett, with two men from each company as guards. The regiment was consequently not ready for immediate combat parachute duty.

b. The Regiment had khaki tropical uniforms, similar to the uniforms worn by English colonial troops.

c. As soon as it arrived in France, the Regiment had received the following order:

"In all telephonic conversations and in all verbal and written orders, the Company should be called Battalion, the Battalion should be called Regiment, and the Regiment should be called Division: This is all for the purpose of fooling the enemy as to our strength."

d. On the Channel coast, the 5th Regiment had enormous quantities of munitions. The 3d Battalion alone had at

Avranches 65 tons of different munitions, including many mines.

e. On June 18, 1942, the equipment of the regiment in heavy weapons was far from being complete. It especially lacked heavy mortars and most of its allotment of AT rifles.

f. About June 15, 1942, the following rumor circulated in the Regiment, "The 2d Battalion is leaving for Libya immediately." By June 18, nothing had happened to confirm this rumor.

g. Since its arrival in France (on May 20, 1942) the 5th Regiment had received 60 Russian ponies which were to be trained to be dropped by parachutes from special airplanes, with opening bottom.

## 8. SPECIFIC INFORMATION CONCERNING THE 3D BATTALION:

Component companies:

- 9th Co (Rifle) - Capt. Baeker
- 10th Co (Hv Wpn) - 1st Lt. Kiar
- 11th Co (Rifle) - 1st Lt. Christufek
- 12th Co (Hv Wpn) - 1st Lt. Hohge

Ground transportation of the companies: In June 1942 each company had drivers assigned, one chauffeur per motorcycle and one chauffeur and one assistant chauffeur per other vehicle. Men other than trained parachutists had to ride in vehicles requisitioned on the spot, for the normal transportation available consisted of 1 Opel passenger vehicle (with AA pedestal for twin machine guns), 4 motorcycles with side-cars, and 10 trucks of such varying makes as Opel, Diesel, and Ford:

- 1 Trk, Co Office
- 1 Trk, Ord Workshop
- 2 Trks, Am
- 1 Trk, Bag (wearing apparel and equipment)
- 1 Trk, Bag (food for 1 day)
- 2 Trks, Ki (two rolling kitchens and provisions)

- 2 Trks, Cargo (parachutist transportation)

## 9. MISCELLANEOUS SUPPLEMENTARY INFORMATION:

a. The Regiment should theoretically have been equipped (but was not, up to June 1942) with 1 smoke-shell mortar platoon of 40 men, and 1 communication platoon of about 40 men having radio transmitters and receivers with a range of about 40 miles.

b. The cannon company was armed with 9 infantry cannon of 105-mm caliber.

c. The antitank company had six 37-mm AT guns and six 20-mm AA guns. (The latter were rapid-fire cannon with magazine.)

d. The battalion should theoretically be equipped (but was not, up to June 1942) with 1 communication platoon of 30 men with radio transmitters with a range of about 8 miles.

The company should theoretically be equipped (but was not, up to June 1942) with 2 small flame throwers with a range of about 38 yards. The several companies were equipped with radio transmitters of a type normally allotted to platoons (with a range of about 8 miles).

# APPENDIX C

## GERMAN PARACHUTES

German parachute troops use at least three types of parachutes: marked RZ1, RZ16, and 36DS28. The RZ16, which was invented and first constructed at Cologne, has been in service since the beginning of 1941, and, because it opens without shock, is fast becoming the preferred type.

Parachute equipment is divided into four main parts: the parachute proper (or canopy and rigging lines), the containing bag and pack, the harness, and the accessories.

The parachute itself consists of a silken (or substitute material) canopy made up of a certain number of panels, each panel cut in the shape of a thin isosceles triangle with the apex removed. (See fig. 9.) Each of the three types has 28 panels. Each panel has 4 gores (tapered sections), cut from a single piece of material in such manner that warp and weft are both at an angle of 45 degrees to the long axis of the panel. Panels are

*A cheery Fallschirmjäger display a captured British bren gun.*

numbered serially in the lower corner, number 1 carrying in addition the special markings of the parachute. These are the manufacturer's stamp or trademark, which includes type, mark number, weight, date of manufacture, and identification number; the manufacturer's inspection mark, giving the date of the last factory inspection; and the Air Ministry stamp which gives the date of the Air Ministry inspection.

In a German parachute with 28 panels there are 14 rigging lines which pass through the top vent. The lines are continued down through the seams on opposite sides of the canopy and then run as free lines to the lift webs. Each line is 21 meters (69 feet) long, so that with a canopy 62 square meters (648 square feet) in area, there are some 5 to 6 meters (16 to 20 feet) of free rigging line on each side, between the periphery of the canopy and the lift webs.

When packed, the canopy and rigging lines fold inside the bag, which is fastened by means of a ring to the static line. The bag is then contained within the pack, which consists of a base (next to the man's back) and four flaps which close over the bag. A further bag, in which the whole parachute is kept during shipment, is included among the accessories, and is removed when the person enters the plane.

The harness is made of webbing and consists of a belt with a large buckle in front, two braces, two thigh straps, and a strap across the top of the chest. It is connected to the rigging lines by hemp lift webs. Each web is so made that its lower end forms an eye which fits into the appropriate "D" ring of the harness, where it is secured by a screw, the free upper ends being joined to form two eyes. To each of the four eyes so formed, seven rigging-line ends are attached.

The parachutes are automatically opened by a static cord, 6 meters (20 feet) long, fastened to the inside of the plane. which pulls the bag away from the pack, releasing the canopy. The cord then becomes detached, taking the bag with it. After a drop of some 80 feet the parachute has become completely operative and the subsequent falling speed of a man and parachute is about 16 feet per second. The shock felt by the parachutist when he reaches the ground is comparable to that transmitted by a jump without parachute of from 16 to 18 feet.

*Figure 9. German parachute construction*

A. Apex in which catch lines are joined.
B. Apex seam.
C. Separate panels comprising a section.
D. Elastic joints that give elasticity to parachute.
E. Diagonal seams joining the individual panels of a radial section.
F. Radial seams that bind sections together.
G. Bottom seam that gives firmness to parachute bag and forms its lower edge.
H. Catch lines stretchable 25% when new.

A piece of silk as it comes from the weavers to the cutting room. If the procedure shown here were followed, only the threads running vertically would be touched. In order to prevent this, the cutting is done as shown below.

By cutting the silk in this manner (lowest panel of a section), the resistance to tearing is doubled. All the seams of the parachute are sewn fourfold and are said to be absolutely secure.

# APPENDIX D

## THE DROPPING OF GERMAN ARMS CONTAINERS

The standard German arms containers are all dropped in a more or less similar manner. The parachute is attached to one end, which has a cylindrical projection slightly smaller in diameter than that of the body of the container and is 4 inches deep. Inside this ring there are two brackets or handles for the attachment of the parachute lines. It is not known for certain what device is used for obtaining a quick opening of the parachute, but it is believed that there is some small explosive charge fitted with a fuze giving a few seconds delay. The other or lower end of the container is reinforced by radial stiffening ribs which end in a circular flange about 1½ inches deep by 15 inches in diameter. The size of the parachute is such that containers fall at an approximate speed of 26 feet per second (18 miles per hour). To take the shock of falling on hard ground at this speed, they are provided with a shock absorber screwed into or clipped to the circular flange at the lower end. This is a cylinder, 15 inches in diameter by approximately 18 inches deep, made of some light metal of the appearance of aluminum and corrugated. When the container lands, this metal cylinder is crushed and thus absorbs the impact; it can be replaced if and when the container is dropped again.

For transporting on the ground, the containers are provided with four carrying handles, two on each side. They can also be mounted on a pair of balloon-tired bogie wheels and two or more can be towed one behind the other. For this purpose a trailing arm is fitted, which, when not in use, folds back into the container. The bogie wheels are apparently carried in the container itself ready for use on landing.

The containers are equipped on the inside with special devices for holding various types of equipment and supplies. A special carrier which hangs inside of the main container on straps is used for delivering small arms. All these carriers or holders are designed for quick release to facilitate recovery of arms and ammunition from the container by the parachute soldier in the shortest possible time.

The standard containers are carried inside the plane and released probably from a specially adapted bomb rack, at the same time as the parachutists themselves. The faster rate of fall of the containers insures that they arrive on the ground first. (It is also contended that containers are either dropped as bombs after parachutists have dropped or else one container is dropped after every third parachutist.) In dangerous areas, however, some containers may be carried by aircraft less defenseless than the Ju-52, such as the Ju-88 or the He-111.

# THE GERMAN AIR ATTACK ON CRETE

## *Tactical and Technical Trends,*
## *No. 8, September 24, 1942.*

In any study of defense against air-landing and air-borne attack, the more important lessons are those from Crete. The German conquest of this island in May 1941 is as yet the chief instance of success in a purely air-landing operation, against determined resistance, without the effective cooperation of forces employing surface transport either by land or sea. The usual primary objective of such operations is the capture of one or more airdromes through which air-landed troops can be poured in to swamp the local defense, and this has nowhere else been successfully done.

### TERRAIN

Crete is about 3,320 square miles in area, and of irregular, elongated shape, with an east-to-west length of 160 miles and a north-and-south width varying between 7 1/2 and 35 miles. Most of its surface consists of mountains whose upper slopes are snow-covered throughout most of the year. The highest peak rises to nearly 8,000 feet. As in most Mediterranean regions, the lower slopes are largely, although not wholly, deforested. The climate is of Mediterranean type, hot at midday, followed by an acute drop in temperature towards sunset and the nights are cold.

The population in 1928 was just under 400,000. Most of the people live in a narrow strip along the north coast, along which runs the main road of the island. This strip also includes the 3 principal towns which are (from west to east): Canea with about 27,000 people, Retymno with about 9,000, and Candia (also called Herakleion) with about 33,000. The 3 air fields were near these towns: at Maleme, on the alluvial fan of a creek on the north coast about 10 miles west of Canea; at Retymno (a landing

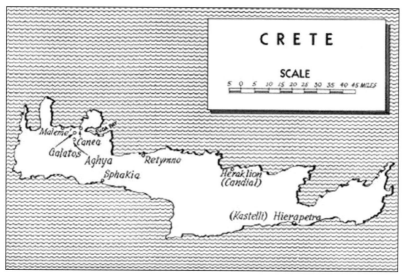

*Sketch No. 1*

strip); and at a point about 4 miles east of Candia. A small auxiliary field was being constructed in May 1941 at Kastelli-Hierapetra in the southeastern part of the island.

The only sheltered harbor for large ships, the fine natural anchorage of Suda Bay, is also on the north coast between Canea and Retymno and somewhat nearer to the former. The one south-coast anchorage showing on the Admiralty chart is the imperfectly sheltered roadstead of Sphakia, almost due south of Suda. The harbor at Candia is shallow and artificial, and there is no shelter for vessels either at Canea or Retymno (see Sketch No. 1). The air distances in statute miles going due east along the north coast are about as follows: from the west end of the island to Maleme, 14 miles; from Maleme to Canea, 10 miles; from Canea to Retymno, 25 miles; from Retymno to Candia, 35 miles; and from Candia to the east end of the island, 66 miles. Thus from Maleme to Candia the total distance is 70 miles.

This 70-mile north-central coastal strip was to be the combat zone. In it the small and fertile alluvial lower valleys are often covered with old olive groves affording good cover from air observation.

## STRATEGIC SITUATION

The position of Crete with reference to surrounding areas (see Sketch No. 2) made it easy for the Axis to attack, difficult for the British to hold, and important to both. On the recently conquered Greek mainland, the Greek islands, and the Italian Dodecanese Islands, the Axis had a large number of airdromes within easy flying range to the northwest, north, and northeast. The nearest, on the Greek mainland at Molaoi about 30 miles north-northwest from Cape Malea, is only about 93 miles from the northwestern point of Crete, and about 105 miles from Maleme. The field on the island of Melos is only about 93 land

*Sketch No. 2*

miles north of Suda, and that at Naxos about 135 miles northwest of Maleme. The fields in Rhodes the most distant of the Italian-owned Dodecanese Islands, are only about 220 miles east-northeast from Maleme. Numerous and well-established fields lay further back on the Greek mainland at Argos and Corinth in the southern part of Greece, and at Meneidi, Eleusis, and other fields near Athens.

By contrast, the British had to reinforce, if at all, over far greater distances: 240 miles from Tobruk to Maleme, 340 from Mersa Matruh, 460 from Alexandria, and about the same distance from Cyprus. Thus, even with equal air numbers the Germans would have had the advantage, and with their greatly superior numbers they had complete air supremacy.

The importance of Crete to both sides lay in its geographical position. In British hands it furnished a base from which they could bomb the Roumanian oil fields, then the only natural source of oil for Germany. Furthermore, the island was a possible stepping-stone to the Balkan mainland, helped to prevent German isolation of Turkey, facilitated the movements of the British Mediterranean fleet, and correspondingly cramped not only operations of the Italian fleet but also all east-west coastwise shipping in Greek waters, since for the moment the Corinth Canal was blocked. With the island in German hands the situation would be reversed, and in addition Axis supply routes to Italian Tripolitania would be relieved from an additional threat.

## BRITISH PREPARATIONS

The general situation in late April was that the British, having occupied Crete in November 1940 and having subsequently intervened on the Greek mainland with a force of less than 40,000 men, had suffered a defeat in which about a third of this force had been killed or captured and the remainder had been evacuated, most of them with very little equipment.

On Crete, there were about 37,500 British and Allied troops,

*Fallschirmjäger flying to Crete.*

most of whom had been evacuated from the mainland and had taken part in the campaign in Greece. British troops numbered 23,500; about 4,000 were Palestinian and Cypriot labor troops; and some 10,000 were Greek troops, including local militia. As a result of its heterogeneous character and loss of vital equipment (including even mess kits), this force was far weaker in fighting strength than the figures would indicate. Another difficulty was the fact that commanders in Crete had been so frequently changed (three times in April) that continuity in preparations for defense had been impossible. The last appointment of Major General Freyberg, came on April 28.

The ground defensive works had been improvised by the local British commanders with scanty means and according to doctrines that varied with the individuals concerned. Since it was evident that the airports would be the chief German objectives, defenses were chiefly grouped around the Maleme and Candia fields. A New Zealand brigadier afterwards said that the English officer responsible for the defense of Maleme had laid out too fixed and rigid a scheme, and one too easily visible from the air. By contrast, the defenders of the Candia-Herakleion field were better concealed and were flexibly disposed in depth, with most of them held out for counter-attack.

General Freyberg's late arrival allowed him little time in which to rearrange the field fortifications. However, a German officer, describing the campaign, acknowledged the skill of the new British commander's troop dispositions, especially the concealment of the New Zealanders in the old olive grove near Aghya prison, about 8 miles east of Maleme and about 3 miles southwest of Canea. In general, Freyberg's leading idea was to protect the airfields and to deny them to the enemy, posting his troops so that the German parachutists, whose attack he correctly anticipated, must land on a defended area within striking distance of one of his detachments.

On or shortly after May 1, the British became certain that the Germans would soon strike. The opinion of the 3 British services was therefore asked as to whether Crete should be held. All 3 thought the chances slim. The RAF had only 42 serviceable planes on the island, and the British air strength in the whole Middle East was very limited. The Navy considered missions in Cretan waters without adequate air support to be suicidal.

Freyberg said he would fight in any case, but thought the position hopeless without full air and naval support.

Against the 42 British planes, the Germans were about to attack with nearly 800 bombers and fighters, 500 transport planes, and 75 gliders. Thus, with the RAF strength negligible before May 19, and wholly absent after that date, the ill-assorted and ill-equipped 37,500 British and Greek troops on the ground were to contend unaided against about 35,000 German air-landing troops backed by overwhelming air support.

The naval aspect may be summarized by noting that the powerful British Mediterranean Fleet succeeded in preventing Axis small-boat landings during the decisive phase, but only at the price of losses so great that, had the fleet not been withdrawn, control of the Mediterranean might have passed to the Italians. The Royal Navy contributed to the ground action only in an indirect way by diverting German air strength; on the decisive day, May 22, there was a lull in the bombing of British ground forces because German bombers were attacking the warships.

## GERMAN PREPARATIONS

The German Intelligence made mistakes which might have affected the outcome of the operations. Most serious was their idea that all British troops evacuated from Greece had gone to Alexandria rather than to Crete; this led to estimate of Allied strength on the island as 3,500 - less than a tenth of the real numbers. Other German miscalculations were that no Greek troops were on the island, and that a considerable portion of the islanders were pro-German. Nevertheless, German energy and flexibility were to succeed in spite of a wholly inaccurate intelligence estimate.

The German attack, including preparations, falls into four clearly marked phases, which suggest a possible pattern of air-landing operations. First, reconnaissance and the establishment of air supremacy; second, air bombardment, including machine-gun strafing; third, seizure of one or more fields by air-landing

*The aerial bombardment of Crete.*

attacks; and fourth, exploitation of the air-landing attack by pouring in air-landed reinforcements. The third phase is usually the decisive one. The phases interlock: reconnaissance continues through the operation, and air bombardment continues throughout both seizure and exploitation.

The timetable of the Cretan operations is as follows: organized British resistance on the Greek mainland having ceased approximately on April 30, phase 1 (reconnaissance of Crete), began on May 1 and continued for 10 days accompanied by light dive-bombing and strafing. On May 10, phase 2, that of heavy air bombardment, began and was most successful. Phase 3, that of air landings, was begun on May 20, ending late on May 22 with the clearing of Maleme airport and its neighborhood of the British. On May 23, phase 4, exploitation by normal air landings, was begun, and on the night of May 31 the last organized British evacuation ended.

For about a month before May 20 there had been a general German movement south. Transport planes and gliders gathered near Athens and Corinth. Special troops came by air, sea, road, and rail. Supplies and stocks of munitions were accumulated. Advance landing fields near Crete, on the Aegean Islands of

Naxos and Melos, and in the Peloponessus at Molaoi, were hastily constructed.

Air photography on Crete began about May 1 and continued until May 10, accompanied by light dive-bombing and strafing. The German plan for the main attack was based upon abundant air photographs, and from them the assaulting troops were carefully instructed as to the terrain and British positions. German prisoners taken during the main attack were well provided with good sketch maps.

From May 11 to 17 inclusive, there was daylight bombing and strafing of increasing frequency and intensity. By May 18, German air action had reduced the serviceable British aircraft to three Hurricane fighters and three Gladiator fighters at Candia, and one Hurricane at Maleme. Since they were contending against odds of nearly a hundred to one, and seem to have had no good shelter on the ground, this tiny remnant was flown to Egypt on May 19 - which happened to be the day before German air landings began.

The crews of the British anti-aircraft guns suffered severely from lack of adequate concealment, most of them were driven from their gunpits after firing only a few rounds. Contemporary press reports spoke of one gunner who knocked down a number of German dive bombers by holding his fire until each had dropped its bomb and flattened out; thus the gunner did not give away his own position. Often, however, groups of three German pilots would dive on a British gun positions simultaneously from different angles, so that one or two of the group would be attacking the gun in the flank or rear while it was being aimed at the third.

From May 17 to 19 inclusive, air bombing and strafing were further intensified in order to break the defender's morale. Attacks on the Maleme and Candia airdromes were especially heavy and frequent. Heavy air attacks were also directed at the one good British debarkation point, Suda Bay, which became a graveyard of ships. During May 18 Suda was heavily attacked seven times by dive bombers with fighter support. The effectiveness of the air attacks on British shipping may be judged from the following figures: of 27,100 tons of supplies shipped from Egypt only 2,700 tons (10%) were successfully unloaded, 3,400 tons (12.5%) were sunk, and 21,000 tons (77%) had to be returned to Egypt because it was not practicable to unload them between 2300 and 0300 - which was the only period when unloading could safely take place. At least 14 cargo ships were sunk at Suda.

Having thoroughly reconnoitered, interrupted supply, beaten down the slight air resistance, and partially worn down the ground defenders, the Germans attacked with airborne troops at dawn on May 20.

## THE ATTACK: MAY 20

The dawn attacks of May 20 struck the Maleme-Canea area, especially at Maleme, where some defenders claimed the intensity of the 90-minute preliminary bombardment exceeded any artillery preparations of 1914-18. Gliders landed west of the airdrome under cover of the dust cloud raised by the air bombardments, and parachute troops promptly began landing behind them and on the airdrome itself. The New Zealanders made eight successful bayonet charges, but were constantly driven back by intense bombing and strafing, and during the night of May 20-21 withdrew one-half mile eastward. The airdrome however was still under artillery fire.

Also at dawn, 1,800 glider troops and parachutists landed southwest of Canea. Here, a New Zealand brigade with some crack Greek troops had been well concealed and entrenched among olive trees. The fighting in this area was intense, and a German officer states that the heaviest German losses occurred here. By nightfall all Germans in the area had been mopped up, except those in a strongly walled prison at Aghya, which they organized defensively, using the labor of the prisoners.

*The drop zone during the attack.*

At Retymno, German parachutists landing at 1600 had been cleared from the airdrome but had held nearby, and had captured some field guns and two tanks.

Candia, also attacked at 1600 but ably defended in depth from well-concealed positions, held well, and all parachutists who landed within the airdrome perimeter were killed.

Astonished but not discouraged by the unexpected strength of the garrison and by their own heavy losses - the British estimated they had killed 80 percent of the parachute troops who had landed - the German High Command decided to throw in their whole air-landing strength.

In the attack phase which opened on this day, most of the offensive work on the ground was done by parachute troops. However, in this instance, such troops were preceded by the landing of glider troops.

The reasons of the Germans for having the first air-landed troops come in gliders were that the silent approach of the motorless planes might achieve surprise, and that if unmolested by the defenders these light aircraft would land safely on almost any terrain. Also, their passengers could leave them fully equipped and therefore ready for almost instant combat, whereas parachute troops on landing are at first nearly helpless, and remain below their full combat value for some time.

Parachutists are not only helpless while descending but also during the first half minute after landing. They are more or less helpless during the first two minutes and still very vulnerable throughout the first five minutes. If their arms containers are captured or covered by fire they cannot fight. Consequently prompt counter-attack by the defenders, even when far inferior in numbers, is often successful.

On the other hand German gliders are vulnerable in the air because most of the ammunition, instead of being carried on the men or packed in strong and comparatively small containers as in the case of parachute troops, is packed together in the fore part of the glider where it will explode if hit, destroying both the ship and all on board. Moreover the slow speed of the glider as compared with a motored plane makes it comparatively easy to hit on the wing.

The mission of the glider troops was to cover the first parachute landings.

The first parachutists to land followed the gliders closely. The parachutists had the normal objectives of such troops - to seize airfields and to disrupt the defender's communications, thus preventing defensive movements and counter-attacks.

The German parachutists who landed in Crete were organized not merely in single companies attached as advanced wards to normal air-landing divisions as in Holland, but in an organic "division" - we might call it a reinforced brigade - of three regiments.

Tactically the parachutists were light infantry with considerable small-arms fire power but with no heavy weapons and only a few medium-heavy ones. Their method was that of "vertical envelopment," divided into a holding attack and main attacks as in envelopments on the ground. The main attacks are intended to seize an objective; the holding attacks are made by smaller groups who divert the enemy from concentrating on the main attack and cut his communications in order to prevent him from counter-attacking. On the ground, parachutists are relatively immobile since they have no transport except what they may be able to seize.

Thus the main attack against Maleme came from the west, the parachutists landing behind an advance guard of glider troops. Meanwhile, two smaller parachute groups landed farther east in rear of the defenders. Another main parachutist attack was aimed southwestward against the Galatos-Aghya position west and southwest of Canea, with a glider group and two small parachute groups landing in the defender's rear.

A German account claims that the British expected the main attack to fall upon Retymno and Candia, but there is no evidence of this in British accounts of their dispositions.

## THE ATTACK: MAY 21

The second day, May 21, went somewhat in favor of the British except at Maleme. There, and on the nearby beaches, planes attempted in the morning of May 21 to land normally, or to crash-land, with troops, guns, and motorcycles. Heavy German losses resulted, especially from artillery fire, but at 1615, 500 fresh parachutists landed behind the airdrome defenders. On the same day, May 21, an attack by reinforced parachutists from Aghya against Galatos was repulsed. At Retymno the British counter-attacked, cleared the airdrome, and retook their captured guns and tanks, but were unable to destroy other groups of parachutists who had cut the road both east and west, and had been reinforced. The town of Candia and its airdrome were held after bitter fighting, and only Maleme seemed insecure.

## THE ATTACK: MAY 22

On the third day, May 22, two New Zealand battalions at Maleme attacked with bayonets and reached the airdrome after fierce fighting, but could not hold the airfield in daylight against 400 unopposed German dive-bombers and fighter planes. Fresh

Germans continually landed.

Late on May 22 the turning point was reached. Despite the extreme fatigue of the troops - a number of units had made up to 20 bayonet charges - Freyberg decided on a last desperate attack to retake Maleme airfield. Before this attack could be made, however, reinforced German troops from Aghya succeeded in moving north and cutting the communications between the British defenders of Maleme and those in the Canea-Galatos area. Retreat of the Maleme defenders had to be ordered; Maleme field became a secure German operational base; the decisive phase of the attack ended; and the phase of German exploitation of victory began.

## EXPLOITATION: MAY 23 to MAY 31

Throughout May 23 Retymno held. Shortages necessitated a 30 percent cut in rations, and medical stores were also insufficient.

On May 24 the Germans further intensified their air attacks, brought in fresh troops by air, and prepared to attack the Galatos position held by the New Zealanders. During the night of May 24-25, a commando force originally intended to lead a counter-attack against Maleme was successfully landed at Suda by destroyer, but the situation had so deteriorated that this force had to be used as a rear guard. General Freyberg judged that his tired troops could not hold much longer. Nevertheless, when about 2000 on May 25 the Germans broke through the Galatos position of the New Zealanders and took Galatos village, two greatly fatigued New Zealand battalions charged with the bayonet and retook the village; General Freyberg considers this charge one of the great efforts in the defense of Crete.

From May 26 to the last naval evacuation from Sphakia on the night of May 31, the British mission was to save as many troops as possible. That they were able to save 14,580 (53 percent) of the British garrison of 27,500, was because German air attacks slackened. Continuation of intensive attacks, so British officers estimated, would have meant practically

*The graves of Fallschirmjäger killed in the batttle for Crete.*

complete destruction of the British garrison.

The defenders of Candia were in control of the local situation and considered themselves victorious until ordered to evacuate on the night of May 28. The seizure of Maleme airdrome had been decisive. The loss of a single airdrome meant eventual defeat everywhere in Crete.

# THE MASSACRE OF KONDOMARI

During the morning of 20 May 1941, German paratroopers of the III Battalion of the 1st Air Landing Assault Regiment were dropped southeast of Maleme. Their landing site extended to Platanias and included Kondomari. The invaders were confronted by the 21st and 22nd New Zealand Infantry Battalions,and they were joined by ill-armed local civilians carrying primitive weapons. The paratroopers experienced strong resistance and suffered severe losses that totaled nearly 400 men, including their commander Major Otto Scherber. Eugen Meindl, the regiment's commander, was shot through the chest and had to be replaced by Oberst Hermann-Bernhard Ramcke.

Throughout the Battle of Crete, the Allied forces and Cretan irregulars had inflicted heavy losses of lives on the Wehrmacht. In particular, the unprecedented, valiant resistance from the local population exasperated the Prussian sense of military order

*Civilian males being selected for massacre at Kondomari.*

according to which no one but professional warriors should be allowed to fight. Reports from General Julius Ringel, commander of the 5th Mountain Division, stated that Cretan civilians were picking off paratroopers or attacking them with knives, axes and scythes. Even before the end of the Battle, unproven and exaggerated stories had started to circulate, attributing the excessively high casualties to torture and mutilation of paratroopers by the Cretans. When these stories reached the Luftwaffe's High Command in Berlin, Göring commanded Student to undertake inquiries and reprisals. Thus, seeking to counter insurgency and before inquiries were complete, temporary commander General Kurt Student issued an order to launch a wave of brutal reprisals against the local population right after the surrender of Crete on 31 May. The reprisals were to be carried out rapidly, omitting formalities or trials and by the same units who had been confronted by the locals.

Following Student's order, the occupants of Kondomari were blamed for the death of a few German soldiers whose bodies had been found near the village. On 2 June 1941, four lorries full of German paratroopers from the III Battalion of Luftlande-Sturm-Regiment 1 under the command of Oberleutnant Horst Trebes surrounded Kondomari. Trebes, a former member of the Hitler Youth, was the only key officer of the Battalion to have survived the Battle unwounded. Men, women and children were forced to gather in the village square. Then, a number of hostages were selected among the men while women and children were released. The hostages were led to the surrounding olive groves and later fired upon in cold blood. The exact number of the victims is unclear. According to German records, a total of 23 men were killed but other sources raise the toll to about 60. The whole operation was captured on film by Franz-Peter Weixler, then serving as a war propaganda correspondent (kriegs-berichter) for the Wehrmacht.

*Aged civilians confronting the fallschirmjäger at Kondomari.*

*These unsuspecting men had no idea that they were shortly to become the victims of the Fallschirmjäger massacre.*

The day following the massacre of Kondomari, forces of the 1st Air Landing Assault Regiment went on to commit yet another war crime, razing Kandanos and executing most of its populace.

After the summer of 1941, Franz-Peter Weixler was dismissed from the Wehrmacht for political reasons. Later on, he was accused of high treason for having leaked uncensored material related to the paratroopers' activities in Crete that included photographs taken in Kondomari, and for having helped some Cretans to flee. Weixler was arrested by the Gestapo, court martialled and imprisoned from early 1944. In November 1945, during Göring's trial in Nuremberg, Weixler gave a written eyewitness report on the Kondomari massacre. His negatives from Kondomari were discovered in the German archives in the early 1980s and his photographs became widely known.

In July 1941, Horst Trebes was awarded the Knight's Cross for his leadership during the assault against Crete. Three years later (1944), he was killed in action in Normandy.

After the surrender of Germany, Kurt Student was captured by the British. In May 1947, he came before a military tribunal

*Horst Trebes (right) with W. Gericke in July 1941.*

to answer charges of mistreatment and murder of prisoners of war by his forces in Crete. Greece's demand to have Student extradited was declined. Student was found guilty of three out of eight charges and sentenced to five years in prison. However, he was given a medical discharge and was released in 1948. Student was never tried for crimes against civilians.

# TESTIMONY AGAINST GOERING, NUREMBERG TRIALS

## Information supplied by Franz Peter Weixler
## Krailling, near Munich, 11 November 1945

In connection with the Nurnberg trials against/Goering et.al., I would like to make the following statement with the express authorization that it may be used in the trial.

I was a prisoner of the Gestapo from January 16, 1944 to April 1945. I had been indicted for treason before the People's Court, and the only reason I was not executed was the fact that my files were destroyed once in Berlin, and once at the Gestapo office in Nurnberg. One of the reasons for my indictment was

*Close up of a soldier pictured during the killings.*

*Paratroopers with Horst Trebes in front being prepared to open fire.*

the fact that I had told friends the truth about the parachute enterprise in Crete in May 1941, and also that I had taken pictures there. I am attaching an "order" of the German Army, which I appropriated and kept, issued by the divisional staff of the Parachute Division, commanded by General Student. I shall now describe the manner in which I was enabled to take the photos mentioned above.

On June 1 or 2, 1941, I was in my billet in the capital of Crete, Chania, when a young officer told me that that afternoon I would see something very interesting. In answer to my question, he told me that a punitive expedition would be sent against several villages since the corpses of parachutists, massacred and plundered, had been found. The supreme command of the Luftwaffe had been informed of this several days before, and an order had been received from Goering according to which the sharpest measures, i.e. the shooting of the male population between 18 and 50 years of age, was to take place. I told the young officer and a (Captain Gericke, that I had never seen a single massacred parachutist, but had seen dozens of dead comrades whose faces had partially decayed because of the tropical heat. I then went to see Major Stenzler who told me that a delegation of the German Foreign Office had left Berlin the day before in order to make an investigation concerning the alleged massacring of German soldiers. I told Stenzler that during the first days of the fighting I had seen vultures pick on the corpses of our comrades. I reminded the major that we had Been innumerable half-decayed comrades, but that we had never Been a single murder or massacre, and that I would consider it outright murder to execute Goering's order. I implored Major Stenzler not to send out the punitive expedition. When he told me that this was none of my business, I went to see Lieutenant Trebes, who was just making a speech to a group of about 30 men, to the effect that "the action would have to be carried through as quickly as possible, as a reprisal for our comrades who had been murdered".

The punitive expedition consisted of Trebes, another lieutenant, an interpreter, two sergeants; and about twenty-five parachutists of the Second Battalion. As a photographer assigned to my division I was permitted to accompany this Kommando. Near the village of Malemes, we stopped and Trebes showed us

*Some of the victims of the Fallschirmjäger attempt to flee from the hail of bullets unleased by Trebes and his men.*

*A pistol armed Fallschirmjäger administers a killing shot to any of the victims of the Kondamari massacre still showing a sign of life.*

the corpses of several soldiers, obviously in the process of decay. He incited the men against the civilian population. We continued our drive to the village of Kondamari. The men got off, and ran into the few houses of the little community. They got all men, women, and children onto the little square. A German soldier brought out the coat of a parachutist which he had picked up in one of the houses, and which had a bullet hole in the back. Trebes had the house burned down immediately. One man admitted having killed a German soldier, but it was not possible to convict any of the others of any crimes or plundering, and I therefore asked Trebes to stop the contemplated action and give us orders to return, taking with us only the one man. Trebes however, gave orders to separate the men from the women and children; then he had the interpreter tell the women that all of the men would be shot because of having murdered German soldiers, and that the corpses would have to be interred within two hours. When Trebes turned hip back for a few moments, I made it possible for nine men to get away. Trebes had the men form a half circle, gave the order to fire, and after about fifteen seconds, everything was over. I asked Trebes, who was quite pale, whether he had realised what he had done, and he replied that he had only executed the order of Hermann Goering, and avenged his dead comrades. A few days later he received the Knights Cross from Goering for his "braveness" in Crete.

It was possible for me to get the negatives of my photos to a friend in Athens, who saved copies for me. In spite of the fact that the original film was taken away from me by my superiors, and that I had to sign a declaration to the effect that I had no copies, it was possible for me to save copies and use them later in my activity against Hitler and his regime.

# LESSONS FROM CRETE IN ANTI-PARACHUTIST TACTICS

## Tactical and Technical Trends, No. 8, September 24, 1942.

The following account of the parachutist attack on Crete is based on a report of a British junior officer who commanded a light anti-aircraft unit during the attack on that island. The ideas expressed are those of the officer concerned, based on his own experience, and are not to be taken as official. Moreover, since this operation, certain developments have taken place in the tactics used by parachute troops.

The attack on Candia started on May 20 with a heavy air bombardment which lasted for 2 hours. At the end of this time the Ju-52's carrying parachutists arrived on the scene and proceeded to drop their cargo. The procession came in three waves, one to the east of this sector, another to the west, and the third one over the center.

The reporting officer stated that "those dropped on the central sector dropped right on top of my gun position, with the result that my small party of 25 men had to deal with vastly superior numbers of parachutists.

"We did more than deal with them, however. We almost completely destroyed them, for if an immediate attack can be made on parachutists the second they leave the plane and touch the ground, they are almost powerless to resist. By capturing and destroying their containers, which carry all their weapons, and by pulling down the distinctively colored parachutes marking the containers and rallying points, we managed to prevent them from getting any weapons and assembling.

"In my experience, the lessons that we learned were the following:

*German paratroopers jumping from Ju.52s over Crete.*

"Speed of action - you must attack them with all your available forces, however small, at the earliest possible moment, i.e., as soon as they leave the plane.

"Destruction or capture of containers and rallying points.

"By either confining them to the smallest possible area, or by widely dispersing them into small pockets, prevent them from getting supplies.

"By strict and careful camouflage, try to make them land on top of you, for the closer to a defended locality they descend, the less of a menace they become."

The mission of parachutists may be the creation of diversions, harrassment, occupation of key points, or the destruction of certain definite objectives such as factories, radio stations, anti-aircraft batteries, fire-control stations, and the like.

There is always a preliminary aerial bombardment. During this bombardment the carriers approach in formation. The bombardment ceases, and the parachutists jump at heights between 300 and 500 feet. The individual parachutists land with quite a bump. Some of them are badly winded. Some have difficulty in managing their parachutes. Others may even be dragged by their parachutes. It takes an appreciable length of

*Max Schmeling, the heavy weight boxer, was a celebrity recruit into the ranks of the Fallschirmjäger.*

time to get clear of their parachute harness; then a dash is made for the arms containers which have also been dropped in parachutes, usually of a distinctive color. After the containers are opened and the arms obtained, some little time is required to rally and assemble into units.

The parachutists have a definite objective, and everything else is disregarded. In cases where a definite objective may not have been set, or where possibly a drop was not made in the right place, harrassing positions are quickly found, such as houses, trees, shrubbery, corn-fields, ditches, and sunken roads.

Intercommunication and communication between air and ground was amazingly good. After landing, contact was continuously maintained with reconnaissance aircraft by the use of Very lights, flags, and radios.

Once on the ground and collected into units, the parachutists became rather immobile, light infantry with a very high fire-power. However, as the descent is made with only limited supplies, there is a time limit to the firepower if supplementary ammunition supplies are not received.

Parachutists land with food and supplies for 48 hours. Fresh supplies are dropped in the same manner as were the parachutists. The same type of aircraft is used, and they approach in the same formation as in the actual parachute attack, dropping supplies in the occupied areas daily. Reinforcements are dropped by parachute to assist units in difficulty.

Anti-Aircraft artillery and pursuit-aircraft assistance is of course invaluable for the defending forces, but, as in Crete, may not always be available.

Camouflage of ground positions is most important. Troop positions, particularly anti-aircraft or field artillery positions which can be identified from the air, will be subjected to merciless air bombardment.

Troop positions should be provided with slit trenches. These should be inconspicuous, and loose soil should be disposed of so as not to attract attention.

Strong points should be selected and organized for all-round fire; if possible, they should be so situated as to give mutually supporting fire.

Strong points and other positions should be wired in, but a small gap should be left to enable the garrisons to make rapid sorties to attack the parachutists promptly during the first vulnerable minutes. Such gaps should be closed with trip wires provided with bells, or tin cans that rattle, in order to provide a warning to the garrison.

When the troop carriers arrive and are dropping or about to drop parachutists, effective results can be obtained with light automatic weapons by firing at the doors of the aircraft. In general, rifle fire should be held until the parachutists hit the ground, when they become sitting targets. This is especially so with troops who are not specialists in the use of the rifle. However, particular men known to be first class shots may be given permission to "pot" the parachutists during their descent.

It is essential to attack the parachutists with all automatic arms, rifles, and bayonets immediately upon landing. Pistols did not prove particularly effective in Crete.

The time factor is of the greatest importance:

For 30 seconds after landing parachutists are incapable of action.

For 2 minutes they are more or less helpless.

From 3 to 5 minutes before they can get organized, they are very vulnerable.

Certain men must be detailed whose sole job is to collect or destroy arms containers and their contents.

(Note: Although not mentioned by this officer, other officers who served in Crete have stated that British troops, particularly service units, who were not well armed with automatic weapons, were able to do very well with the German submachine guns which they took away from parachutists or got out of captured containers.)

Another squad should be detailed to recover and hide (or destroy) the colored parachutes which are used to mark arms containers, rallying points, officers, etc. Colors vary with each attack. In this officer's opinion, submachine guns, rifles, or bayonets are the best weapons with which to attack parachutists. Revolvers were not of much use (the soldier who is a well-trained pistol shot is a rarity).

A supply of hand grenades is very useful for dislodging parachutists from houses and strong points.

Each defensive strongpoint should be self-contained, with plenty of ammunition and food and water for several days - 7 to 10 days emergency rations.

Every unit and subunit from base workshops to front-line troops, every man - infantry, artillery, cook, or clerk - must have a job to do and know it perfectly. There must be no spectators - no neutrals.

The time factor cannot be overemphasized.

Each unit must be drilled and officers must have in mind

several tentative plans. It is most difficult to guess beforehand exactly where the parachutists are going to land, so probably a very simple plan in the nature of a rough outline is best. But in his mind's eye, the commander must visualize every possible form of attack so that in the 30 seconds after the drop begins, he knows exactly what he is going to do.

Dispose of the first batch of parachutists as quickly as possible, as they are nearly always followed by a second batch who come down in greater force in the same area, probably about an hour later.

As soon as they land, kill everybody possible. Confine the remainder in the smallest possible area. Confuse the enemy aircraft as much as possible by firing captured Very pistols and laying out captured signal flags. (After a little experimenting with captured Very pistols isolated British units in Crete discovered the signals that brought food. As the German air transport system was quite efficient these units did not go hungry.)

When the enemy are dropping supplies, send out patrols to capture or destroy these supplies. Or, if this is not possible, cover the areas where supplies have been dropped by machine-gun or artillery fire.

Tanks are invaluable for mopping up.

Don't waste men.

Isolate them, starve and smoke them out.

# AIRBORNE OPERATIONS: A GERMAN APPRAISAL

# PREFACE

This study was written for the Historical Division, EUCOM, by a committee of former German officers. It follows an outline prepared by the Office of the Chief of Military History, Special Staff, United States Army, which is given below:

1.  a. A review of German airborne experience in World War II.

    b. An appraisal of German successes and failures.

    c. Reasons for the apparent abandonment of large-scale German airborne operations after the Crete operation.

2.  a. German experience in opposing Allied and Russian airborne operations.

    b. An appraisal of the effectiveness of these operations.

3.  The probable future of airborne operations.

It is believed that the contributors to this study (listed on page iv) represent a valid cross-section of expert German opinion on airborne operations. Since the contributors include Luftwaffe and Army officers at various levels of command, some divergences of opinion are inevitable; these have been listed and, wherever possible, evaluated by the principal German author. However, the opinions of Generalfeldmarschall Albert Kesselring are given separately and without comment wherever they occur in the course of the presentation.

The reader is reminded that publications of the GERMAN REPORT SERIES were written by Germans and from the German point of view. Organization, equipment, and procedures of the German Army and Luftwaffe differ considerably from those of the United States armed forces.

This study is concerned only with the landing of airborne

*A gruesome close up photograph of dead Fallschirmjäger in the back of a truck, Chambois, France 1944.*

fighting forces in an area occupied or controlled by an enemy and with the subsequent tactical commitment of those forces in conventional ground combat. The employment of airborne units in commando operations, or in the supply and reinforcement of partisans and insurgents, is not included in this study, nor is the shifting of forces by troop-carrier aircraft in the rear of the combat zone. Such movements, which attained large size and great strategic importance during World War II, should not be confused with tactical airborne operations.

# THE CONTRIBUTORS

Generalmajor (Brigadier General) Hellmuth Reinhardt, committee chairman and principal author, was Deputy Chief, General Army Office, 1941-43, and later Chief of Staff, Eighth Army, on the southern front in the Ukraine and Romania.

Contributors on German airborne operations:
- Generalleutant (Major General) Werner Ehrig, operations officer of the 22d (Army Air Landing) division during the attack on Holland.
- Oberst (Colonel) Freiherr von der Heydte, an outstanding field commander of German parachute troops, author of the "Appendix."
- Generalfeldmarschall (Field Marshal) Albert Kesselring, commander of the German Second Air Force during the Netherlands campaign, and later Commander in Chief, Southwest.
- General der Fallschirmtruppen (Lieutenant General) Eugen Meindl, regimental commander during the attack on Crete, later airborne division and corps commander.
- Generalleutant (Major General) Max Pemsel, Chief of Staff, XVIII Corps, which included the ground forces committed in the attack on Crete.
- Generaloberst (General) Kurt Student, the chief of German parachute troops during the entire war.

Contributors on Allied airborne operations, and on German defense measures against them:
- General der Infanterie (Lieutenant General) Guenther Blumentritt, Chief of Staff, OB West.
- Oberst (Colonel) Albert Emmerich, G-3, German First Army.
- General der Flakartillerie (Lieutenant General) August Schmidt, in 1944 commander of Luftgau VI, which provided the mobile troops to combat Allied airborne landings at

Nijmegen and Arnhem.

- General der Kavallerie (Lieutenant General) Siegfried Westphal, the chief of staff of OB Southwest in Sicily and Italy, and later of OB West.
- Oberst (Colonel) Fritz Ziegelmann, G-3, 352d Infantry Division.

*A Fallschirmjäger mortar team in action.*

*Paratrooper with rifle, pistol, stick grenade and ammunition belt in Tunisia, near the Algerian border 1943.*

# FOREWORD

## BY GEN. FRANZ HALDER, CHIEF OF STAFF
## OF THE GERMAN ARMY, 1938-42

I concur completely with the ideas of the principal author of this study, which are presented on the basis of his collaboration with the most experienced German specialists.

In view of the present state of technical development, I place a considerably higher estimate on the opportunities for airborne operations in a war between military powers than does the principal author. The latter considers that the essential conditions for the successful use of airborne operations-even on a large scale-exist only in close cooperation with the operations of ground troops.

Assuming that there are sufficiently strong air forces and air transport facilities, I believe that in the future airborne landings by large bodies of troops (several divisions under unified command) can also be used for independent missions, that is, for such military operations as are not closely related in place and time with other ground actions, but are only bound to the latter by the general connections existing between all military operations in the theater of war. It is precisely along these lines that I envisage the future development of airborne warfare. I am convinced that with the proper preparation and present-day technical facilities it is possible to form new military bases by means of large-scale airborne landings far in the enemy's hinterland, in areas where he expects no threat from ground troops and from which independent military operations of large scope can be undertaken. To supply by air such large-scale airheads for the necessary time is essentially a technical problem which can be solved. The independent commitment of large airborne forces seems to offer a present-day high command an effective means for suddenly and decisively confusing the enemy's system of warfare.

Future wars will not be confined to the customary military fronts and combat areas. The battle fronts of opposing ideologies (resistance movements, revolutionary partisan organizations, Irredentist elements), which today in an age of dying nationalism cut through all great powers and civilized nations, will be able to create favorable conditions for large-scale airborne landings deep in the enemy's country and for maintaining such bases of operation as have been won by airborne operations in the interior of the enemy's sovereign territory. To prepare the people in these territories in time and to make them useful in war will be the task of these forces, under a unified command, to which the language of our time has given the name of the "Fifth Column."

# CHAPTER 1

# GERMAN AIRBORNE OPERATIONS IN WORLD WAR II

The Germans carried out airborne operations on a large scale only twice in World War II; once in May 1940 in Holland, and again in May 1941 in connection with the occupation of Crete. Accordingly, German experiences are based in the main upon these two operations which took place during the first years of the war and which constituted the first large-scale airborne operations in the history of warfare. Although there were no other major airborne operations launched by the Germans, the German command, and in particular the parachute units which continued to be further improved during the course of the war, seriously concerned themselves with this problem. Two other cases are known in which plans and preparations for large-scale airborne operations progressed very far, namely, the intended commitment of parachute troops as part of the landing in England (Operation SEELOEWE) in 1904, and the preparations for the capture of the island of Malta in 1942. Neither of these plans was carried out.

Airborne operations on a smaller scale were carried out against the Greek island of Leros in 1943 and during the Ardennes offensive in 1944. The experience of minor operations such as these, as well as the trials, tests, and research done by the airborne troops during the war, are also discussed in this study.

The problems encountered in German airborne operations have been divided into three categories:

Planning airborne operations from the point of view of the higher command, designation of objectives for air lands, and cooperation with ground troops, the Luftwaffe, and the naval forces;

Actual execution of an airborne operation; the technique and tactics of landing troops from the air; and

Organization, equipment, and training.

In addition, a number of specific points and recommendations have been attached in the form of a appendix contributed by Col. Freiherr von der Heydte, who may be regarded as the most experienced field commander of German airborne troops.

In every air landing there are two separate phases. First the strip of terrain must be captured from the air; that is, an "airhead" must be established. This airhead may, or may not, include the objective. Second, the objective of the air landing must either be captured or held in ground battle. The second phase is similar in nature to conventional ground combat, if we disregard the method used to transport the troops and the factors of strength and supply which are influenced by the circumstances that all communication is by air. The first phase, however, has new and unique characteristics. Troops committed during the first phase require special equipment and special training. In limited engagements such troops can also carry out the missions connected with the second phase. For large-scale operations regular ground troops will have to be used in addition to special units. These ground troops need equipment modified to fit the conditions of air transport.

In recognition of these factors the Wehrmacht (German Armed Forces) had taken two steps even before the war. In the 7th Airborne Division of the Luftwaffe, a unit had been created whose mission it was to capture terrain by parachute jumps and landing troop-carrying gliders. An Army unit, the 22d Infantry Division, had been outfitted for transport by air and given the designation of "Air Landing Division."

Both of these units were committed during the first great air-landing attack in Holland in 1940, at which time the 22d Infantry Division had to be reinforced by elements of the 7th Airborne

Division to capture the initial airhead. On the other hand, smaller missions, such ass that to capture Fort Eben Emael, were accomplished by troops of the 7th Airborne Division without assistance from other units. During the attack on Crete a year later, it was impossible for the airborne troops to achieve a victory alone. It was only when Army units transported by air had arrived that progress was made toward capturing the island. Since it had not been possible to transport the 22d Infantry Division to Greece in time, the 5th Mountain Division, already in Greece, had to be employed, a measure which proved to very successful. Preparations lasting approximately one month were sufficient to prepare the division for the new assignment. The special equipment of the mountain troops was suited both for transport by air and for commitment in the mountainous terrain of the island.

## Section I. PRINCIPLES OF EMPLOYMENT

The airborne operations undertaken by the Germans during World War II may be classified in two groups, according to their purpose. In the first group, the attack took the form of sending an advance force by air to take important terrain features, pass obstacles, and hold the captured points until the attacking ground forces arrived. This operation was aimed at a rigidly limited objective within the framework of a ground operation which was itself essentially limited. This was the case in the airborne operation in Holland in 1940 and, on a smaller scale, at Corinth in 1941 and during the Ardennes offensive in 1944. The common characteristic of all these operations is that they were limited to capturing the objectives and holding them until the ground forces arrived. Beyond that, there was no further action by the troops landed from the air, either in the form of large-scale attacks from the airhead or of independent airborne operations. At the time, such missions would have been far beyond the power of the troops committed.

In the second group are the operations having as their objective the capture of islands. On a large scale these included the capture of Crete in 1941; on a more limited scale these included the capture of Leros in 1943. Crete came closer to the concept of an independent operation, although the objective was strictly limited in space. The planned attack on Malta also belongs in this category. The experience of World War II shows that such missions are well within the means of airborne operations.

Two considerations influence the selection of the objective in airborne operations. The first is that in respect to their numbers, and also as far as their type, equipment, and training is concerned, the forces available must be fit for the task facing them. This is of course true of all tactical and strategic planning, but at the beginning of the war, because of a lack of practical experience, the manpower needs were greatly underestimated.

The second consideration-and this is especially important for airborne operations-is that at least temporary and local air superiority is an absolute necessity. This factor has a decisive influence upon the selection of the objective, at least as far as distance is concerned. The latter condition prevailed during the large-scale German airborne operations against Holland and Crete; but the first condition did not exist in equal measure, a fact which led to many crises. both were absent during the unsuccessful Ardennes offensive.

In preparing for an airborne operation the element of surprise must be maintained. In the operation against Holland surprise was easily achieved since it was the very first time that an airborne operation had ever been undertaken. Once the existence of special units for airborne operations and the methods of committing them had become known, surprise was possible only through careful selection of time and place for the attack, and of the way in which it was started. This requires strict secrecy regarding preparations. In the Crete operation such secrecy was lacking, and the grouping of parachute troops and transport squadrons became known to the enemy who had little doubt as to their objective. The result was that the German troops landing from the air on Crete came face to face with an enemy ready to defend himself; consequently, heavy losses were sustained.

*[Field Marshal Kesselring's comments on the element of surprise:*

*Airborne operations must always aim at surprise, which has become increasingly difficult but not impossible to achieve. Detection devices, for example radar equipment, can pick up air formations at a great distance and assure prompt counter-measures. Flights at very low altitude, such as were planned for the attack against Malta, are difficult to detect by means of such equipment. The effectiveness of these devises is neutralized by natural barriers in the terrain. Attention can be diverted by deception flights, and confusion is often caused by suddenly changing the course of the aircraft during approach runs, as well as by dropping dummies at various places behind the enemy front. Night operations increase the possibility of surprise,; in many cases this is also true fro the ensuing ground combat. It is impossible to overestimate the value of soundless glider approaches during twilight hours for the successful execution of air landings. It is easier to preserve secrecy in the assembly of airborne units than in concentrations prior to ground operations of the same size, since with proper organization the airborne troops can be assembled and attacks prepared deep in friendly territory within very short periods of time. Crete is the classic example of how this should \*not\* be done.]*

Connected with the element of surprise is deception. A typical deceptive measure in airborne operations is the dropping of dummies by parachute. Both sides availed themselves of this measure during World War II. Experience shows that an alert enemy can soon recognize dummies for what they are. A mingling of dummies and real parachutist promises better result because it misleads the enemy as to the number of troops involved and leaves him guessing as to where the point of main effort of the attack is to be located and as to where only a diversionary attack is concerned. As an experiment, the German parachute troops also attempted to equip the dummies with smoke pots which would start smoking when they reached the ground, thus making it still harder for the enemy to see through the deception. This idea never advanced beyond the experimental stage.

Careful reconnaissance is also of special importance in airborne operations. The difficulty is that in airborne operations troops cannot, as in ground combat, conduct their own reconnaissance immediately in advance of the main body of troops. In attacking, their spearheads penetrate country that no reconnaissance patrol has ever trod. This is why reconnaissance will have to be carried out very carefully and well in advance. Military-geographical descriptions, aerial photography, reports from agents, and radio intelligence are sources of information. All this requires time. Before the Holland operation enough time was available, and it was utilized accordingly. Reconnaissance before the Crete attack was wholly inadequate and led to serious mistakes. For instance, enemy positions were described as artesian wells and the prison on the road from Alikaneos to Khania as "a British ration supply depot." Both the command and the troops had erroneous conceptions about the terrain in Crete, all of which could have been avoided if more careful reconnaissance had been made.

Several views were current among German airborne commanders as the best way of beginning an airborne operation. One method, which General Student recommended and called "oil spot tactics," consisted in creating a number of small airheads in the area to be attacked-at first without any definite point of main effort-and then expanding those airheads with continuous reinforcement until they finally ran together. These

*Following the Allied bombing the Fallschirmjäger moved in to take up defensive positions during the battle for Cassino.*

tactics were used in both Holland and Crete. General Meindl, on the contrary, was of the opinion that a strong point of main effort had to be built up from the very onset, just as was done in attacks made by the German panzer forces. However, no German airborne operations were launched in accordance with this principle. Neither of the two views can be regarded as wholly right or wrong; which one will prove more advantageous will depend on the situation of one's own and the enemy's forces, terrain, and objective. Even in conventional ground combat an attack based on a point of main effort which has been determined in advance is in opposition to the Napoleonic method of "on s'engage partout et puis on voit" (one engages the enemy everywhere, than decided what to do). This implies, however, that a point of main effort will have to be built up eventually by committing the reserves retained for this purpose. If the relatively strong forces required by this method are not available, it would be better to build up a point of main effort from the very beginning. On the other hand, since in airborne operations a thrust is made into terrain where the enemy situation is usually unknown, the "oil spot method" has a great deal in its favor. For example, it breaks up enemy counter-measures, as in the attack on Crete. During the initial attack there, parachute troops were distributed in a number of "oil spots;" there were heavy losses and no decisive successes. No further paratroopers were available and the decision was made to land the troop carriers of the 5th Mountain Division wherever an airfield was in German hands, even though it was still under enemy fire. This was taking a great risk, but the plan succeeded from this point onward, the island was captured and the other "oil spots" liberated. At one time, the whole operation was within a hair's breadth of disaster because the airheads, which were too weak and too far apart, were being whittled down. After the decision to attack one point had been carried out and had succeeded, the remaining "oil spots" were useful since they prevented the enemy from moving his forces about freely. The advantages and dangers connected with this method are clear.

The unavoidable inference from the Crete operation is that commanders of airborne troops should land with the very first units so that clear directions for the battle can be given from the outset. The over-all command, however, must direct operations from the jump-off base and influence the outcome by making a timely decision as to where a point of main effort should be built up, and by proper commitment of reserves. For this purpose an efficient communication system and rapid reporting of the situation are necessary.

Since the actual fighting in airborne operations takes place on the ground and in general is conducted in close touch with other ground operations, it is advisable to have both airborne and ground operations under the same command. In the German airborne operations in Crete, the Luftwaffe was in command and neither the ground force commanders in Greece nor the OKH (Army High Command) had anything to do with the preparations; this is a mistake.

In airborne operations the air forces are responsible for keeping the air open for the approach and supply of the landing formations. They also aid in the operation by reconnaissance and by commitment of their tactical formations in preparing the landing and in supporting the troops which have landed. In this they must receive their orders from the command of the ground forces.

*[Field Marshal Kesselring's comment on command for airborne operations:*

*I do not agree with the statement about the conduct of airborne operations. These operations must be considered from the viewpoint of the Armed Forces High Command (OKW). The commander in chief of a theater, for example the Eastern Theater or the Southern Theater, is also a joint forces commander with a joint staff. He is responsible for all airborne operations which*

*A group of Fallschirmjäger in action with specialist artillery.*

*are launched within his theater. Hence, the commander of the airborne operation must also be subordinate to him. This commander will generally be an officer of the Air Force whose staff must be supplemented, according to the task assigned him, by Army and Navy officers as well as airborne officers. In some special cases and invariably in those cases where there is no direct connection with the ground and sea fronts, the OKW will plan the operation and conduct it directly. The situation and the mission would probably be the decisive factors in making a decision about the chain of command. If the mission involves supporting a ground attack by means of an airborne operation directly behind the attack front, the army group will be given the over-all command, will assign missions, and will intervene whenever necessary for the purpose of air-ground coordination. As soon as the attacking ground troops establish an effective link-up with the airborne unit, the airborne troops will be brought into the normal chain of command of the attacking ground forces. Unit of command takes precedence over all other considerations. Until that time the airborne troops are commanded by their own unit commanders. The highest ranking officer in the landing area commands at the airhead and is himself subordinate to the commander of the airborne operation- in the above case to the army group commander-who works in close coordination with the Air Force commander. In all other cases where, as in Holland, Crete, Oslo, there are no direct connections with operations of the Army or the Navy, a special headquarters, preferably commanded by an Air officer and staffed with Air Force personnel, should be placed in charge of the operations. In appropriate cases, it will be the Air Force commander concerned, especially if the tactical air support units for the airborne operation have to taken from his sector of the fighting front. This commander's responsibilities include not merely the landing of the first echelon but also the considerably harder problem of directing the following waves and modifying their landing orders in accordance with the development of the situation at the airhead. They also involve the preparatory bombing attack; protection by reconnaissance planes, bombers, and close-support aircraft aimed, I might say, at supporting the ground troops with high and low altitude attacks carried out by the extended arm of a flying artillery; the air transport of supplies; and finally the evacuation by air of casualties, glider pilots, and other specialists. The shortest possible chain of command is decisive for success.]*

Mention has already been made of the fact that control of the air is an essential prerequisite for airborne operations. If that control is widespread and based upon maintaining the initiative in air combat, the air support of the airborne force will present few problems. Airborne operations based upon temporary and local air superiority are also possible, but they make strenuous demands upon the attacker's air force. Immediately before an operation, the enemy's forward fighter fields must be rendered useless, and all anti-aircraft installations along the route selected for the flight must be neutralized. Enemy radar and communications facilities in the area should also be put out of action, and any enemy reserves near the projected airhead must be subjected to intensive bombardment. Such activity must begin so late that the enemy will have no time to bring in additional troops or to repair the damage.

Each airborne formation will require a fighter escort. From the point of view of air tactics, it will therefore be desirable to keep the number of formations or waves to a minimum. The primary mission of the escort will be to protect the troop-carrier aircraft against enemy fighter planes, especially during the landing and deployment of the troops for ground action. The neutralizing tactics already mentioned will have to be continued during and after the landing to insure the sage arrival of supplies and reinforcements. The troops on the ground will continue to require air support to take the place of artillery that would normally be supporting them.

Throughout World War II the German parachute troops had the benefit of close cooperation on the part of the Luftwaffe reconnaissance. The main problem was to see to it that the parachute troops received good aerial photographs and, if possible, stereoscopic pictures of the area they were to attack so that they could familiarize themselves in advance with the terrain. It proved to be advisable to distribute stereoscopic equipment down to battalion level and to send members of the parachute units to the aerial photography school of the Luftwaffe for special training in the use and interpretation of stereoscopic pictures. In this way, it was possible to offset to a certain degree the lack of terrain reconnaissance prior to an airborne attack.

Finally, the air forces support the airborne operation by attacking the enemy's ground forces. During the war all German airborne operations took place beyond the range of German artillery, and only in the case of the Ardennes offensive were parachute troops to be supported by long range artillery bombardment. This plan was never put into operation because the radio equipment of the forward observer assigned to the parachute troops failed to function after the jump. Ground strafing and preparatory bombing of the landing area proved to be the best solution everywhere. Air attacks upon enemy reserves being rushed toward the airhead can be of decisive importance because of the extra time gained for the troops which have been landed. Opinions are divided, however regarding the value of direct air support of the troop fighting on the ground after their landing. On Crete, formations of the Luftwaffe's Von Richthofen Corps solved this problem in exemplary fashion. Other experiences, however, would seem to indicate that it is impossible to support airborne troops, once they are locked in battle, by delivering accurate fire from the air or well-placed bombs. Lack of training and inadequate skill in air-ground cooperation may have disastrous effects. Systematic training, in which well-functioning radio communication from the ground to the air and coordination between formations on the ground and in the air are emphasized, should achieve results just as satisfactory as those achieved between armored formations and air forces. It goes without saying that cooperation from the artillery, in so far as airborne operations are conducted within its range, is worth striving for, both in preparation of the landing and in support of the troops after they have landed. Attention may be drawn to the Allied airborne operation north of Wesel in March 1945 where British and American artillery support is said to have been extremely effective. When airborne operations are effected on a beach, naval artillery takes the place of Army artillery. An increase in range made possible by the development of rockets will result in further possibilities for support.

When troops landed by air are joined by forces advancing on the ground, the airborne operations are conducted against islands and coast lines, junction with amphibious forces has the same effect. In World War II, accordingly, airborne operations were always conducted in coordination with ground or amphibious forces. How soon this junction with ground or amphibious forces will be effected depends upon the number of troops and volume of supplies, including weapons and equipment, ammunition, rations, and fuel, which can be moved up by air. This again depends upon the air transport available and upon control of the air to insure undisturbed operation of the airlift required for this purpose. If such relief cannot be provided in time, the troops landed will be lost. So far, no way has been devised of fetching them back by air. In the German airborne operations of World War II, supplying troops by air over long periods of time was impossible, not only because control of the air could not be maintained, but also because of a lack of transport planes. In German doctrine, the guiding principle was that as much airlift was needed to resupply a unit which had been landed by air with ammunition and weapons (excluding rations) for a single day of hard fighting as had been necessary for the transport of the unit to the drop point. While this fighting does not take place at all times and be all elements at the same time, consideration must be given to the fact that in addition to supplies it will be necessary to bring up more troops to follow up initial successes and give impetus to the fighting. Eventually, the troops will need to be supplied with additional rations and, if they break out of their airheads, with fuel. In this field, too, postwar technical achievements offer new possibilities. During the war the Germans believed that junction of an airborne formation with ground troops had to be effected within two to three days after landing. On the basis of conditions prevailing in those days, these deadlines consistently proved to be accurate in practice.

## Section II. AIRBORNE TACTICS

Three methods were used during World War II to land troops from the air at their place of commitment. Troops could be landed by parachute, by transport gliders released from tow planes, or by landing of transport planes. All three methods were used in varied combinations, depending upon the situation. In accordance with the lessons derived from World War II, the last method, for reasons which will be discussed later, is unsuitable for the initial capture of enemy territory from the air, that is, the creation of an airhead. Accordingly, only the commitment of paratroopers and gliderborne troops will be discussed here. (German experiences in the technique and tactics of these two methods are described in detail in the appendix.) The advantages and the disadvantages of the two methods will be compared here and conclusions drawn as to their future use.

Commitment of gliders has the great advantage that they land their whole load in one place. Since debarkation is a matter of seconds, the troops can bring their full fire and striking power to bear immediately after landing. The almost noiseless approach of the gliders, which have been released from the tow planes far from the objective, increases the element of surprise. Furthermore, diving gliders are able to make very accurate spot landings within a limited area. Glider troops are also able to open fire with aircraft armament upon an enemy ready to repulse them. German parachute troops were convinced that this would have an excellent effect on morale. In practice the method was used only once, so far as is known, and that was on a very small scale in July 1944 at Vassieux against the French maquis, but its success was outstanding. While the glider offers pronounced advantages during the first attack on an objective which is defended, in the subsequent phases of the airborne operation its advantages over the use of parachutes lie in the fact that it can deliver substantially greater loads, such as heavy weapons, guns, tanks, and trucks.

On the other hand, parachute jumps make it possible to drop very large numbers of troops at the same time within a certain area. Moreover, until the very last minute the commander can alter his selection of the drop point. He can accordingly adapt himself to changed conditions far more easily than is the case with gliders. The latter are released far from the objective and once this has been done there is no way of changing the landing area.

On this basis it will be seen that the glider is particularly suited for the capture of specifically designated and locally defended objectives, such as Fort Eben Emael, while parachutists are more effective for the purpose of capturing larger areas. Among the German airborne troops a marked preference developed for a method in which an initial attack by gliders was quickly followed up by mass parachute jumps. This plan is not, however, universally applicable. In each case methods will have to be adapted to the situation, terrain, type of objective, and amount of resistance to be expected from the enemy; the commander of the parachute troops will have to make his decision within the framework of his mission.

*[Field Marshal Kesselring's comments on the relative merits of parachute and glider landings:*

*The comparative advantages and disadvantages of parachute and glider landings are well described. Nevertheless, I maintain that at least the same concentration of forces can be achieved with a glider landing as with a parachute jump. Experience shows that parachute landings are very widely scattered, so that assembly takes considerable time. Gliders, according to their size, hold ten to twenty or even more men, who immediately constitute a unit ready for combat. If the landing area is fairly large-the condition of the terrain is of little importance-and if the unit is well trained, the assembly of strong fighting units in a small area will not present any difficulties.]*

A weakness in the commitment of gliders is to be found in the fact that once they have been used they are immobilized on the ground and-at least on the basis of German progress by the end of the war-cannot be used twice during the same operation. The German conclusion was that transport planes had to be used as soon as possible. There is no doubt, however, that in time a way will be found to get the gliders back to their base, for example, by the addition of light engines, or the use of helicopters.

*[Field Marshal Kesselring's comment on re-use of gliders:*

*The abandoning of gliders should not be considered a great disadvantage. Their construction is very simple and within the means of even a poor nation. Excessively complicated devices [for glider recovery] should be avoided. But this does not apply to the development of new types of air transport facilities, especially for peacetime and training requirements, which can perhaps also be used in particularly favorable military situations.]*

It is important to clear the landing zone immediately so that more gliders can land in their turn. When large-scale glider landings in successive waves are to be made, special personnel will have to be provided for the purpose.

It must be mentioned in this connection that German gliders, patterned on those used in sport, had so-called "breaking points" (Sollbruchstellen), that is, joints of purposely weak construction, which would break first in crash landings or collisions with natural or artificial obstacles. This method brought about a substantial economy in construction of the gliders and simplification in procurement of spare parts and maintenance.

## Section III. PARACHUTE TROOPS

The necessity of having airborne units for the initial commitment during air landings has been recognized. In both Holland and Crete elements of Army units, in part by design and in part because of ignorance of the situation, were landed from transport planes in territory still occupied by the enemy or situated within sight of enemy artillery observers. This was recognized as a mistake resulting in serious losses. The only thing that saved the planes landing on the Maleme airfield in Crete from being completely destroyed by direct enemy fire was the fact that the ground was covered with dust as a result of drought and that the planes actually landed in clouds of dust.

During the following war years, the parachute troops in Germany were steadily increased and improved. In accordance with the situation and the nature of their intended mission, the troops had to be trained for commitment either by parachute jumps or by transport gliders. The designation of "parachute troops" (Fallschirmtruppe) and "parachutists" (Fallschirmjaeger) given these units in Germany is accordingly not quite accurate. Fundamentally a major part of the German airborne force was suited for transport-glider commitment only, since the plans of training them as parachutists could not be carried out. In practice, the percentage of trained parachutists steadily decreased with the result that, as the war continued, these troops were almost exclusively used in ground combat. The Wehrmacht, because of the scarcity of manpower, found it impossible to keep these units in reserve for their special duties. It is evident that only the "rich man" can afford such forces, and that efforts must be made to withdraw these troops as soon as possible after each airborne commitment. Otherwise their value as special units will rapidly decrease, something very hard to remedy.

One fundamental lesson derived from the first air landing was that even the very first elements reaching the ground must be fully equipped for battle. The parachutists landing on Crete had nothing but their pistols and hand grenades, the remaining weapons and ammunitions being dropped separately in special containers. After the Crete operation this was changed. It was realized that both parachute and transport glider troops must reach the ground as combat units ready for action. They must have heavy weapons, and especially, tank-destroying weapons adapted to this type of transportation, as well as a suitable type of organization for even the smallest units, making it possible for each to fight independently. (Detailed information regarding the equipment of German parachute troops is contained in the appendix.) In order to capture a usable airhead for the air-

*Dead Fallschirmjäger near Cerantan in Normandy 1944.*

transported units, the parachute troops, over and above the initial landing, must be able to capture airfields, or at least terrain suitable for landing air transports, and to push back the enemy far enough from these areas to avoid the necessity of landing within range of direct enemy gunfire. In other words, the parachute troops must be capable of attacks with a limited objective, and of holding the captured terrain. Consequently, the parachute divisions were equipped with all heavy weapons and artillery; and an airborne panzer corps was organized with one panzer and one motorized infantry division. However, organization of these units never got beyond the initial activation as conventional ground troops, and all plans to use them for airborne landings remained in the theoretical stage. After the Crete operation no German parachute division was committed in airborne operations as a whole unit. The airborne panzer corps never even received adequate training. Only parts of the remaining parachute divisions, of which there were six in 1944 and ten or eleven at the end of the war in 194, were trained for airborne operations. General Student gives a total figure of 30,000 trained parachutists in the summer of 1944. Most of them were in the 1st and 2d Parachute Divisions, of whose personnel 50 and 30 percent respectively were trained parachutists. Commitment of the divisions in ground combat continually decreased these figures so that parachutists from all units had to be recruited for the airborne attack in the Ardennes offensive. In the main, the training of these troops was inadequate. For instance, only about 20 percent of the parachutists committed in this action were capable of jumping fully equipped with weapons. This was a serious disadvantage because very few of the weapons containers dropped were recovered.

Accordingly, the Germans had no practical experience in large-scale commitment of parachutists with really modern equipment, nor was it possible to test the organization and equipment of such formations in actual combat.

Earlier German experience points to two important considerations. In the first place, the parachute troops will be in need of a supply service immediately after landing. On the basis of the Crete experience, it would seem advisable to incorporate service units in the first waves of parachutists. The greater the scale of the airborne operation, the more thought will have to be given to the matter of motorized supply vehicles. Today their transportation in transport gliders presents no technical difficulties. In the second place, in cases where the intention is to follow up initial jumps with the landing of great numbers of air-transported troops, engineer units will have to be assigned to the parachute troops at an early stage for the purpose of preparing and maintaining landing strips for transport planes.

Even though the German parachute troops lost their actual purpose in the last years of the war, they preserved their specific character in the organization of their personnel replacements. The operations actually carried out proved that the special missions assigned to parachute troops call for soldiers who are especially aggressive, physically fit, and mentally alert. In jumping, the paratrooper must not only conquer his own involuntary weakness but upon reaching the ground must be ready to act according to circumstances; he must not be afraid of close combat; he must be trained in the use of his own and the enemy's weapons; and, finally, his will to fight must not be impaired by the privations occasioned by such difficulties in supply as hunger, thirst, and shortage of weapons. For this reason, it is advisable for the parachute troops to take their replacements primarily from among men who have volunteered for such service. The excellent quality of the replacements which the German parachute troops were able to obtain until the very end explains why, even in ground combat, they were able to give an especially good account of themselves.

Good replacements, however, require careful training in many fields. Every paratrooper must be given thorough training in infantry methods, especially in close combat and commando tactics. This was shown to be necessary in all the operations undertaken. Only when the paratrooper proves from the outset to be superior to the attacking enemy can he be successful. Specialist training in the use of various arms and special techniques is essential. A mistake was made by the Germans in separating the initial jump training from the rest of the training program. Instead of becoming the daily bread of the paratrooper, jump practice accordingly evolved into a sort of "special art." All artificiality must be avoided in this branch of training.

Special emphasis must be placed on training officers for the parachute troops. One of the experiences derived from actual operation is that the officers must be past masters in the art of ground combat. The fact that the German parachute troops originated in the Luftwaffe caused a great many inadequacies in this respect. On the other hand, the parachute officer must have some knowledge of aviation, at least enough to be able to assess the possibilities of airborne operations.

There is no doubt that a sound and systematic training program for the parachute troops demands a great deal of time and that in the last years of the war the German parachute formations no longer had this time at their disposal. However, the time required for training, combined with the high standards set for the selection of replacements, acts as a deterrent to their commitment. The higher command will decide to make use of the troops only when all preconditions for a great success are at hand or when necessity forces it to do so. To commit these troops in regular ground combat is a waste. Commitment of parachute divisions in ground combat is justified only by the existence of an emergency. Once the divisions are committed as ground troops they lose their characteristic qualities as specialists.

## Section IV. AIR TRANSPORTED TROOPS

The original German plan to use Army troops for this purpose and to equip and train them accordingly was abandoned early in the war. The 22d Infantry Division, which had been selected in peacetime for the purpose, participated in airborne operations only once, in Holland in 1940. It was found that their double equipment-one set for regular ground combat, the other for use in air-landing operations-constituted an obstacle; consideration for their special mission limited their employment for ground combat. When a fresh commitment in line with their special mission became a possibility in Crete, it was found impossible to bring them up in time. On the other hand, as early as the Norway campaign, mountain troops were flown for commitment at Narvik without much prior preparation. While in this case non-tactical transport by air was involved, the previously mentioned commitment in 1941 of the 5th Mountain Division in the airborne operation against Crete took place after only short preparation and was entirely successful.

On the basis of these experiences the idea of giving individual Army units special equipment for airborne operations was abandoned. The German High Command set about finding ways and means to adapt all Army units for transport by air with a minimum of changes in their equipment. The results were never put into practice because after Crete the Germans did not undertake any other airborne operations on a large scale. Crete, however, proved that the German mountain troops, because of their equipment and the training which they had received, as well as their combat methods, were particularly suited for missions of this nature. In the future the goal must be to find a way of committing not only mountain and infantry divisions but panzer and motorized formations in airborne operations. Their equipment and organization for this purpose will depend upon the evaluation of technical possibilities which cannot be discussed in detail here The chief demand which the military must make upon the technical experts is that the changes required for such commitment be kept to a minimum. A way must be found to determine the best method for such a change so that the troops can undertake it promptly at any time.

The lesson learned from German airborne operations in World War II was that air-transported troops can be committed only if the success of landing and unloading is guaranteed by a sufficiently large landing zone. These troops are not suited to the purpose of capturing an airhead. With the exception of the technical details concerned with their enplaning, these troops require no special training. The logical conclusion to be drawn from this lesson is that parachute troops, who capture the airhead, must be increased in number and supplied with more fire power.

# Section V. TROOP CARRIER UNITS

Transporting troops by air to their area of commitment is more or less a matter of transportation alone and in an efficiently organized modern air force presents no difficulty at all. However, the approach flight and dropping of parachute troops is a part of the operation itself and determines its subsequent success or failure. The inconclusive but rather disappointing German experiences in this field have been set down, from the point of view of an airborne field commander, in the appendix. Transport squadrons-including both the transport planes for the parachutists and the tow planes for the gliders are to the parachute troops what horse teams are to the artillery and motor vehicles to the motorized forces. In each case correct tactical leadership for each mode of transport is a prerequisite for the correct commitment of the troops in time and space-consequently, they must be trained jointly. During commitment the transport squadrons must be subordinated to the parachute commanders, who must be trained to give orders to the transport squadrons in correct and systematic form. The ideal solution would undoubtedly be to incorporate the transport squadrons

*Field communication by telephone, Normandy 1944.*

organically into the airborne forces, but this solution is expensive. Lack of sufficient materiel alone made it impracticable during World War II as far as the Wehrmacht was concerned. A compromise solution would be close cooperation in peacetime training. The transport squadrons will have to be made available to the parachute units well in advance of an airborne operation since joint rehearsals are a prerequisite of success. This fact increases the amount of time needed for the preparation of an airborne operation and at the same time endangers the secrecy surrounding the undertaking, because such a grouping of units can give the enemy valuable leads regarding one's intentions.

The most important factor is the selection of the time and place of the jump and of the release of the gliders. This requires very precise orders and is subject to the decision of the commander of the parachutists. Again and again lack of care in this regard resulted in breakdowns during German airborne operations in World War II. Only twice did strict observance of this point result in smooth functioning-during the airborne operations to capture the Isthmus of Corinth in 1941, when the limited scope of the undertaking made it possible to commit transport squadrons having just finished thorough training in cooperation with parachutists; and during the capture of Fort Eben Emael in 1940, when the units participating in the operation had received joint training over an extended period.

The principle of subordinating the transport squadrons to the parachute commanders makes it imperative that the training of these commanders be extended to include flight training.

In this connection mention must be made of the so-called pathfinder airplanes, whose mission in relation to airborne operations at night is described in the appendix. What has been said above also holds good for them. Their proper use is essential for success and demands, above all, skill in navigation in order to calculate timing accurately.

# Section VI.
# REASONS FOR SUCCESS AND FAILURE

In assessing the successes and failures of German airborne operations the following missions are taken into consideration: Holland, 1940; Corinth, 1941; Crete, 1941; Leros, 1943; and Ardennes, 1944. All other commitments of German airborne troops fall into the category of commando operations or of troop movements by air.

Holland, 1940.-On the whole, the airborne operations against Holland, in spite of a number of critical moments and relatively great losses, must be classified as successful. This success was connected not so much with achievement of the tactical objectives, such as the capture of a number of bridges which were important to the attacking ground forces, as with the morale influence exerted upon the enemy by a wholly new method of fighting. The very fact that in this way large forces could penetrate deep behind Dutch defenses at the outset of the fighting undoubtedly broke the resistance of the Dutch and saved the German Army the cost of a serious fight in capturing Holland. Success is attributable mainly to the surprise provoked by this method, which was used for the first time in the history of warfare.

*[Field Marshal Kesselring's comments on airborne operations in Holland:*

*This was the first airborne operation in history and should be treated in somewhat greater detail. The operation was under the overall direction of the commander of Second Air Force. The tactical commander was General Student. His headquarter was divided into a mobile forward echelon, headed by Student in person, and a stationary rear echelon, which was to assume special importance.*

*The operation was divided into the following parts:*

*An operation with gliders alone against Fort Eben Emael and the Maas bridge. With the capture of Fort Eben Emael, the enemy flanking actions against the Maas crossing were eliminated. The capture of the most important bridge guaranteed that the Maas River would be crossed according to plan and thus established the necessary conditions for the coordination of ground and air operations in Holland. The dawn missions succeeded surprisingly well.*

*A major airborne operation by two divisions to capture the Moordijk bridges, the Rotterdam airport, the city of Rotterdam, and the Dutch capital of The Hague and its airfields. Since the second part of the mission (22d Infantry Division-The Hague) was not successful the subsequent operations in the Dutch coastal area failed to take place.*

*The attempt at surprise was successful. Today one cannot even imagine the panic which was caused by rumors of the appearance of parachutists, supported by the dropping of dummies, etc. Nevertheless, the surrender of Rotterdam was the result of the bold actions of the parachutists and the air attack against the defended positions in Rotterdam. The operation had been organized by Student with the thoroughness characteristic of him. In fact, it had been a small military masterpiece, particularly with respect to the following:*

*a. The deployment of troops and troop-carrier formations among the only airfields near the border, just within range of the most distant objectives.*

*b. The incorporation of escort fighter wings in the transport movement, for which General Osterkamp can claim both the responsibility and the credit.*

*c. The coordination of the bomber escort attacks with the landing operations, which had been rendered even more difficult because the commander in chief of the Luftwaffe had ordered an attack against reported enemy naval vessels on the previous evening.*

*The success of the airborne operation with respect to its strategic effect is incontestable. The Dutch Theater of*

*Operations was practically eliminated. The failures and losses can be attributed to the following:*

a. *Interference with the plan of attack by the commander in chief of the Luftwaffe, mentioned above.*

b. *The inadequate strength of parachutists in the air attack group of the 22d Infantry Division.*

c. *Defects in coordination between the 22d Infantry Division and the troop-carrier formations and inadequate training of both in the tactical doctrine for carrying out an airborne operation.*

d. *Technical defects in the signal communications system which made it difficult or impossible for the parachutists and transport formation to cooperate with the 22d Infantry Division and, similarly, hampered General Student in issuing orders to that division.*

e. *The command technique of General Student, who thought of himself as the commander of the Rotterdam operation and thus neglected liaison with the Second Air Force, especially during the most decisive hours.*

*However, all in all, the airborne operation proved successful as the first of its kind because essentially it was correctly organized and carried out with unparalleled verve. It taught us a great number of practical lessons, the application of which did not present any problems which were insurmountable from a technical or tactical point of view. It proved that an airborne operation needs its own command posts, both on the ground and in the air, as well as representation at a higher level.]*

**Corinth, 1941.**-This was an operation on a limited scale undertaken by well-trained parachute troops and troop-carrier units. Resistance was limited. As far as execution of the operation is concerned, it may be rated as a complete success. The actual tactical success was limited to capture of the Isthmus of Corinth. The bridge over the Corinth Canal was destroyed by an explosion of undetermined origin, but makeshift repairs made it possible to use the bridge again that same day. If the attack had been made a few days earlier, the airborne operation, in the form of a vertical envelopment, could have been far more successful and large numbers of the British Expeditionary Force could have been cut off from access to their embarkation ports on the Peloponnesus. It is true, however, that resistance would have been greater in this case.

**Crete, 1941.**-The capture of the island of Crete was the most interesting and most eventful German airborne operation. The initial attack contained all the germs of failure. Only the fact that the defenders of the island limited themselves to purely defensive measures and did not immediately and energetically attack the landing troops saved the latter from destruction. Even though the situation was still obscure, the German command decided to commit its reserves (5th Mountain Division) in an all-out attack against the point which seemed to offer the greatest chances of success; the energetic, purposeful, and systematic commitment of these forces in an attack immediately after their landing changed the threatened failure into a success. A serious disadvantage for the attackers was British control of the sea at the beginning of the operation. Only after several days was it possible to break down this control to such an extent that somewhat insecure communications with the island were possible.

*[Field Marshal Kesselring's comments on airborne operations in Crete:*

*I did not participate in the Crete operation, but later was frequently in Crete, and I have also talked with many parachute officers who were in action there.*

*The special characteristic of this operation was its improvisation. That the objective of the operation was achieved so quickly, in spite of all reverses, is the greatest tribute which can be paid to the fighting men and commanders engaged in it. Improvisation, however, should be avoided if possible, since the* risk involved is too high in proportion to the number of men committed. But it is not true, as stated in this report, that "an airborne operation is ... time consuming ... and affords neither much freedom of maneuver nor a great deal of flexibility."

If the airborne troops have a suitable, permanent organization and if reconnaissance is begun early and carried out with all available means, there is no reason for assuming that an airborne operation cannot be carried out as swiftly as the situation demands. The art of command lies in thinking ahead. Applied to this particular problem, this means the prearrangement of an adequate, efficient ground organization, such as was available in the case of Crete, and the timely procurement of the necessary fuel, etc., via land or sea, which would also have been possible. Under ideal conditions, if permanent large-scale airborne formations had been available, this would have presented even fewer difficulties, since the combat troops would have been flown in by their own transport planes. One can easily conclude from this that a high degree of surprise might have been achieved under the assumed conditions. I repeat, because of the elements of danger inherent in airborne operations, improvisations can be resorted to only in exceptional cases and under particularly favorable conditions. Otherwise they should be rejected.

In this case it would have been advisable for the commander of the airborne operation and, if possible, the division commanders to have made a personal reconnaissance flight to inform themselves about terrain conditions and possible defense measures of the enemy, as a supplement to the study of photographs. The exceptionally unfavorable landing conditions should have induced them to land in a single area away from the occupied objectives with their effective defense fire, and then to capture the decisive points (airport and seaport) intact in a subsequent conventional infantry attack at the point of main effort. In doing this it would not have been necessary to abandon *the use of surprise local glider landings directly into key points, the possession of which would have facilitated the main attack.]*

**Leros, 1943**.-This was an operation on a limited scale which, in spite of some inadequacies in execution, led to success within four days, mainly as a result of a favorable situation and coordination with landings from the sea.

**Ardennes, 1944**.-The airborne operations connected with the Ardennes offensive were definitely a failure. The force committed was far too small (only one battalion took part in the attack); the training of parachute troops and troop-carrier squadrons was inadequate; the Allies had superiority in the air; the weather was unfavorable; preparations and instructions were deficient; the attack by ground forces miscarried. In short, almost every prerequisite of success was lacking. Therefore, it would be wrong to use this operation as a basis for judging the possibilities of airborne operations. At that time the Wehrmacht was so hopelessly inferior to the enemy in manpower and materiel that this operation can hardly be justified and is to be regarded only as a last desperate attempt to change the fortunes of war.

# Section VII.
# GERMAN AIR LANDINGS AFTER CRETE

The airborne operation against Crete resulted in very serious losses which in percentage greatly exceeded those sustained by the Germans in previous World War II campaigns. The parachute troops were particularly affected. Since everything Germany possessed in the way of parachute troops had been committed in the attack on Crete and had been reduced in that campaign to about one-third of their original strength, too few qualified troops remained to carry out large-scale airborne operations at the beginning of the Russian campaign. Air transportation was also insufficient for future operations.

Furthermore, the German High Command had begun to doubt whether such operations would continue to pay-the Crete success had cost too much. The parachute troops themselves, however, recovered from the shock. Their rehabilitation was undertaken and lessons were drawn from the experience, so that a year later a similar undertaking against the island of Malta was energetically prepared. At this point, however, Hitler himself lost confidence in operations of this nature. He had come to the conclusion that only airborne operations which came as a complete surprise could lead to success.

After the airborne operations against Holland and Crete, he believed surprise attacks to be impossible and maintained that the day of successful airborne operations were over. The fact that the Cretan operations came so close to defeat strengthened his opinion. Moreover, the Malta operation would have to be prepared in Italy and launched from there. Prior experience with the Italians had proved that the enemy would be apprised in advance regarding every single detail of the preparations, so that even a partial surprise was impossible. Since Hitler had no confidence at all in the combat value of the troops, which with the exception of the German parachute troops were to be of Italian origin exclusively, he did not believe the undertaking could be successful and abandoned its execution. The special circumstances prevailing at that time may have justified this particular decision, but the basic attitude in regard to airborne operations later turned out to be wrong

According to General Student, Hitler and the commander in chief of the Luftwaffe were so thoroughly convinced that the day of successful airborne operations were over that they believed that not even the enemy would engage in any more large-scale preparations for airborne operations. When the attack by British and American paratroopers on Sicily proved the contrary, the Wehrmacht was itself no longer in a position to carry out large-scale airborne operation. The main essential, superiority in the air, was lacking. The Luftwaffe, no longer a match for the Allied air forces, was unable to assemble enough planes to attain the necessary local superiority in the air and to maintain it for the time required; nor was the Luftwaffe able to make available sufficient transport space. It is true that airborne units were available, but because manpower was so scarce they were constantly being committed in ground operations. The special nature of their mission was retained only to the extent that they were transported by air to point that were threatened and that in some cases, as in Sicily, they were also dropped-by parachute. Aside from this, their training in their special field suffered from a lack of aircraft required for the purpose.

At the time of the Allied invasion of France the commander in chief of the Luftwaffe proposed to link up the planned counter-attack with airborne operations in force. The OKW turned him down because first, the parachute troopers available were already fighting on the ground; second, their training was inadequate for such a purpose; and third, even if the needed troop carriers could be provided, the hopeless inferiority of the Luftwaffe made it impossible to achieve control of the air either in space or in time.

The lesson based upon German operations may then be summarized as follows: In airborne operations cheap successes cannot be achieved with weak force by mean of surprise and bluff. On the contrary, airborne operations which are to achieve success on a large scale require a great outlay of materiel, outstanding personnel, and time for training and preparation. Such operation are accordingly "expensive." From 1941 on Germany, in comparison to its enemies, was "poor".

# CHAPTER 2

# ALLIED AIRBORNE OPERATIONS IN WORLD WAR II

The following discussion is based mainly on three major airborne operations in western Europe-Normandy in June 1944 (the invasion), Nijmegen and Arnhem in September 1944, and north of Wesel in March 1945. The author had little data at his disposal concerning the actions against Allied airborne operations in Sicily in 1943, but this will hardly impair the validity of the following statements, since the airborne landings in western Europe as well as the defense against them were based on lessons of the Sicilian campaign. Any analysis of these operations will therefore cover by implication the earlier experiences in Sicily, so far as they have not been superseded by more recent information.

*[Field Marshal Kesselring's comments on Allied airborne operations in Sicily:*

*The first Allied airborne operations in Sicily preceded the American and British landings by sea. After jumping, the parachutists were scattered over a wide and deep area by the strong wind. Operating as nuisance teams, they considerably impeded the advance of the Hermann Goering Panzer Division and helped to prevent it from attacking the enemy promptly after the landings at Gela and elsewhere. This opposition would not have made itself felt so strongly if General Conrath had not organized his troops in march groups contrary to correct panzer tactics.*

*The second airborne operation of British parachutists took place in the night of 13-14 July 1943, close to the Simeto bridge on the highway between Catania and Lentini. The Commander in Chief, South (OB SUED) anticipated an airborne operation in the Catania plain, even if an amphibious landing were not attempted there. He therefore had ordered that those parts of the plain which were west of the Catania airfield be denied the enemy through installation of wooden obstacles. The antiaircraft units protecting the large airfields in the Catania plain had been specially charged with defense against airborne troops. During the first day of the landing operation, every Allied air landing in the area around Catania could be attacked from the north by reserve of Brigade Schmalz of the Herman Goering Panzer Division and by troops of the 1st Parachute Division, which had been flown in to the eastern coast of Sicily. Even assuming the most favorable conditions for the enemy parachutists, no great Allied success could be expected, at least no success which justified such a large commitment of men. Thus it was inevitable that the British parachute attack in the night of 13-14 July 1943 was crushed. Even their purely tactical success in occupying the Simeto bridge was only of a temporary nature and had no effect on the over-all situation.]*

## Section I. PASSIVE DEFENSE MEASURES

The great latitude which the airborne attacker enjoys in selecting his target makes it extremely difficult for the defender to take passive defense measures against airborne operations. It is quite impossible to set up anti-air-landing obstacles throughout the country. Therefore, no more can be done than to determine what might constitute particularly desirable targets for an airborne attack and in what specific areas air landings directed against these targets might be undertaken by the enemy. These principles were followed by Germany in taking defensive measures against an invasion in the West, since experience Sicily clearly indicated that the enemy would also resort to airborne operations during an invasion. Accordingly, German anti-airborne measures were determined by the following two aims; first, to render useless any points which appeared particularly well suited for landing

*A Fallschirmjäger anti-tank team with Panzerabwehrwaffe, Normandy 1944.*

operations; and secondly, to protect all likely targets against attack by airborne troops.

The first purpose was served by erecting posts approximately 10 feet long and 6 to 8 inches in diameter, imbedded 3 feet deep, connected by wires, and partly equipped with demolition charges. These obstacles were intended to prevent the landing of troop-carrying gliders. German experience showed that such post obstacles are effective only if they are equipped with demolition charges. If no demolition charges are used, although the glider may crash, the enemy will still be able to make a successful landing.

Mining and flooding the terrain were additional measures. The former can be effective against gliders as well as airborne troops if the enemy lands at the very point where the mine field has been laid. However, since such mine fields are necessarily limited because of shortage of materiel and personnel, it is really a matter of luck if the enemy happens to land in a mine field. Furthermore, in the interest of one's own troops, the local inhabitants, and agriculture and forestry, it is impossible to consider extensive application of this method. Undoubtedly, flooding large areas by means of artificial damming deters the enemy from landing at the particular spots. This method, in addition to others, was widely used on the Atlantic coast. Unfortunately, however, at the time of the invasion, some of these flooded areas had dried up again because of lack of rain.

Laying mine fields and flooding areas serve a twofold purpose if, by their location, they not only prevent airborne landings but at the same time constitute obstacles against attack on the ground.

In order to protect potential targets, preparations were made for all-around defense by establishing fortifications, obstacles, and barriers and by wiring bridges for demolition. These are measures which have to be taken everywhere in modern warfare- not only against airborne operations but also against penetrations by mobile forces on the ground, against commando raids, and in occupied territories against partisans and rebels. Wherever they were adequately prepared and reinforced by the necessary personnel, they served their purpose.

Orders for resistance against invasion on the Atlantic coast called for an inflexible defense in which the coast constituted the main line of resistance. To counter any simultaneous large-scale airborne operations, instructions were issued to develop a "land front" several miles inland, with its rear to the coast. In this manner, it was intended to establish a fortified area between "ocean front" and "land front" which was to be defended like a fortress, thus preventing the juncture of the enemy elements attacking from the sea and those landing from the air. During the invasion, however, the Allies did not oblige by landing their troops inland beyond the land front, but landed them either into it or between the two fronts. Furthermore, since the German land front was occupied by insufficient forces because of a shortage of personnel and since it had not been adequately developed, its value was illusory. As a matter of fact, the obstacles, such as flooding, at some points even protected Allied airborne troops against attacks by German reserves.

Experience taught the Germans that passive measures have a limited value against airborne operations. Furthermore, in view of the great amount of time and materiel required, they can be employed only where the fronts are inactive for a long period of time. In mobile warfare, the only passive measures to be applied are preparations for an all-around defense carried out by all troops, staff, supply services, etc., behind the lines.

## Section II. THE GERMAN WARNING SYSTEM

The prerequisite for a successful defense against enemy airborne operations is the early recognition of preparations for such operations. Frequently the signs of imminent air landings may be recognized from agents' reports and radio interception. The Germans themselves had no doubt that the invasion from the West would involve airborne operations on a large scale. On the other hand, it will nearly always remain uncertain up to the last moment, where and when these operations may take place. Changes in the over-all picture obtained through radio interception may appear to give advance warning of an attack. If such changes occur frequently without an actual operation taking place, the alertness of the defender becomes blunted.

The first positive reports are obtained through radar detection of the approach flight. In one case in Normandy it was possible, on the basis of radar, to infer as early as two hours before the jump that an airborne formation was approaching, and to alert the German forces in time.

A well-organized observation service based on the cooperation of all units and agencies, even in the rear areas, should provide assurance that the point where enemy forces are actually landing is quickly determined. All observation, however, is useless unless the reports are rapidly transmitted to the superior agencies and to units immediately concerned. Experience has proved that telephone communications are

*An atmospheric study of a Fallschirmjäger machine gun team in action in the ruins of Monte Cassino.*

unreliable for this purpose since they are frequently disrupted by enemy action, such as preparatory bombing attacks. The transmittal of prepared messages by radio and appropriate warning broadcasts which all agencies and troops are able to receive has proved effective.

As soon as the air-landings are an established fact, the net step is to determine where they are concentrated, which of the attacks are being made for the purpose of diversion and deception, and how wide an area is covered. This is extremely difficult, especially at night, and usually considerable time passes before some degree of clarity is possible. Therein lies the defender's greatest weakness. However, it is never advisable to delay counter-measures until this clarity has been obtained. In most cases, the situation will remain obscure until the counter-attack is launched. It is all the more important, therefore, that reporting should not be neglected during the fighting; this is a matter of training and indoctrination.

It is a unique characteristic of airborne operations that the moments of greatest weakness of the attacker and of the defender occur simultaneously. The issue is therefore decided by three factors: who has the better nerves; who takes the initiative first; and who acts with greater determination. In this connection, the attacker always has the advantage of being free to choose the time and place of attack, and he therefore knows in advance when the moment of weakness will occur, whereas the defender must wait to find out where and when the attack will take place.

The attacker will always endeavor to aggravate the defender's disadvantages by deception and try to force him to split up his counter-measures. As already mentioned in Chapter 1, the most popular method of deception is the dropping of dummies with parachutes. In such cases an immediate attack rapidly determines whether it is a genuine landing operation or a diversion. Radio interception will also prove to be helpful at an early stage, for troops just landed must make prompt use of radio communications to establish contact with each other and with their superior commands at the jump-off base. Radio, however, cannot be used in diversionary actions. Even if dummies were equipped with radio sets functioning automatically or by remote control-which should not be an insoluble technical problem-alert and competent radio interception personnel would not be deceived for long. During the invasion in 1944, it was the signal intelligence service which was able, with comparative rapidity, to give the high command an accurate picture of the enemy's tactical grouping during the air landings. The attacker will naturally endeavor to eliminate any targets such as radar equipment and long-distance radio stations by air attacks prior to the air landings. On the other hand, such attacks can also be an advance warning for the defender.

In occupied territories it is also possible by careful observation and surveillance of underground activities to discover indications of imminent air landings, particularly if counterespionage elements succeed in infiltrating the enemy's network of agents.

## Section III. COUNTER-ATTACK IN THE AIR

Theoretically, the defender's best method of defense against air landings is the employment of air forces to attack the enemy while he is still approaching and to annihilate him or force him to turn back. In 1944-45 during the Western campaign, it was a foregone conclusion that victories were out of the question in view of the hopeless inferiority of the Luftwaffe. To repeat, mastery of the air by the attacking air force will always be the prerequisite for successful airborne operations. The attacker endeavors, by means of bombing attacks, to destroy the defender's air forces on the ground and to protect the approach flight with superior numbers of escort fighters. If the attacker is unable to accomplish this, he will of necessity abandon the idea of an airborne operation altogether. Only in exceptional cases and under particularly favorable conditions will it be possible for the defender to launch an air attack against approaching air formations with any chance of success.

## Section IV. ANTIAIRCRAFT DEFENSE FIRE

A report made in June 1944 by Army Group B on the battle of Normandy includes the following statement: "The designation of areas to be taken under fire by all weapons while opposing the landing of airborne troops has proved satisfactory. (Fire by 20-mm. guns directed at enemy landing forces proved to particularly effective.)" Counter-Measures taken by the attacker include landings at night or during poor visibility. In this connection, the same report says, "Rainy weather and low clouds are favorable for airborne operations, because the planes are able to dive and land without being hit by flak."

It is undoubtedly advisable to inflict the highest possible losses on airborne troops while they are still in the air and while they are landing. To this end, it is necessary for all weapons within whose range an enemy plane is landing to take such a plane under fire. At Arnhem the British troops that landed in the

*A Fallschirmjäger machine gun team with MG.42 in Normandy, 1944.*

vicinity of the Deelen airfield suffered heavy losses inflicted by German anti-aircraft fire. By the same token, however, it true that anti-aircraft fire alone cannot succeed in preventing an air landing, since enemy troops descending by parachute cannot by held off or turned back by overwhelming fire, as might be the case during ground combat. They have to come down, whether they want to or not, and some of them will always succeed in reaching the ground in good fighting condition. It would be a mistake to say that on that account that anti-aircraft defense offers no chance of success. On the contrary, it is the very moment of landing which holds out the greatest promise of success for anti-aircraft defense, for the enemy troops which are landing are without cover; they are defenseless to a certain degree and likely to suffer very heavy casualties. At this juncture, it is impossible for the attacker to protect the troops from the air or by long-range artillery fire. Only gliders can use their arms against the firing defenders, and then only if they happen to be landing at the appropriate dive angle. The losses suffered by airborne troops while jumping and landing will greatly impair their combat efficiency and power of resistance. This will facilitate the task of subsequently annihilating them, and thus frustrate the landing attempt. For instance, the German invasion of Crete illustrates that it is possible to inflict serious casualties by anti-aircraft fire. The same example, however, also demonstrates that the employment of anti-aircraft fire alone is not sufficient to effectively resist an invasion. It can be achieved only through attack. If the defenders of Crete had not contented themselves with using anti-aircraft fire alone but had immediately attacked the troops which had landed, the entire invasion would have failed at the outset.

## Section V.
## COUNTER-ATTACK ON THE GROUND

Experience gained during their own air landings caused the Germans to regard attack as the only effective means of combating airborne operations. Their fight against Allied airborne operations demonstrated the wisdom of this rule. The Germans failed to crush the Allied invasion, not because this principle proved erroneous, but because the necessary forces were either lacking or could not be brought up quickly enough or because German counter-attacks were not conducted properly. In many instances, however, these attacks did impede the progress of Allied airborne operations; at Arnhem they brought Allied operations to a complete standstill.

The most vulnerable period of any air landing is the interval between the jump and assembling of the forces into organized units under a unified command. In order to exploit this weakness, German field service regulations stipulated that any unit within range of enemy troops which had landed from the air should immediately attack since every moment's delay meant an improvement in the situation for the enemy. This method proved to be fundamentally sound. It led to success whenever the enemy landed in small scattered groups or whenever the landing was effected in the midst or in the immediate vicinity of

German reserves ready for action. But these tactics are not successful if the defending forces available for immediate action are too weak to defeat enemy troops vastly superior in number, or if the defenders are too far from the point of landing to be able to exploit the enemy's initial period of weakness. Then there is no longer any purpose in dissipating the defending forces in small isolated attacks or in doggedly fighting the enemy. It now becomes necessary to launch a systematic counter-attack.

Speed in carrying out a counter-attack against enemy airborne troops is essential, because it is certain that the enemy's fighting strength will be increased continuously by means of additional reinforcements brought in by air. In general, only motorized reserves are successful in arriving in time. If the enemy's air forces succeeds, as it did in Normandy, in delaying the arrival of reserves, the chances for success dwindle. The elements which are nearest the enemy have the task of defending important terrain features against air-landed troops, maintaining contact with them, and determining the enemy situation through reconnaissance until all necessary arrangements for the counter-attack have been made. The counter-attack should be conducted under unified command and, as far as possible, launched as a converging attack from several sides and supported by the greatest possible number of heavy weapons, artillery, and tanks; it is directed against an enemy who is well prepared and whose weakness lies merely in that he may be troubled by lack of ammunition and in that his heavy weapons, in general, are inferior in number since he has not established contact with those elements of the invading force which are advancing on land. To prevent the enemy from establishing contact is therefore highly important. If this fails, the defender's chances for success are considerably less. There are no cases during World War II in which the Germans succeeded in annihilating airborne enemy troops after they had established contact with their forces on the ground.

The greatest stumbling block encountered by the Germans in combating Allied airborne operations in the West was the superiority of the Allied air force. German failure to eliminate this air force, or even to clear the skies temporarily, led to the most serious delays in bringing up reserves. The general scarcity of mobile reserves, combined with the fact that they were tied down elsewhere by order of the German High Command, led to the result that in Normandy counter-attacks were made too feebly, too late, or not at all. The success of the German counter-attacks at Arnhem was due to the energetic action and unified command of Army Group B; the fortunate coincidence that two SS panzer divisions were in the immediate vicinity; the weather, which prevented Allied air intervention; and the resistance offered by the German troops at Nijmegen which prevented the prompt establishment of contact between Allied ground troops and airborne elements.

## Section VI. COUNTER-LANDING INTO THE ENEMY AIRHEAD

German specialists in airborne tactics (General Student and others) adhered to the theory that the best defense against an enemy air landing was the launching of airborne operations into the enemy airhead. However, no practical knowledge was gained concerning such operations. During World War II there was only one case in which air landings were effected from both sides in the same area and in quick succession. In 1943 in Sicily, south of Catania, British parachutists jumped into an area where, unknown to the British, German parachutists brought in by air to serve as reinforcements had also jumped a short while before. German reports at hand vary in their appraisal of this incident. One report mentions a complete victory gained by the British troops with heavy casualties among the German parachutists. Another report speaks of the annihilation of the majority of the British paratroopers. What actually happened was that one small

British group did succeed in reaching its objective, the bridge at Primosole, but then lost it. Whether or not this occurred because of or in spite of dual airborne operations can hardly be determined without a more thorough investigation of facts. An air landing into an enemy airhead will always result in confusion on both sides. It will, of necessity, lead to chaotic hand-to-hand fighting, similar to the cavalry battles fought centuries ago, in which ultimately the tougher and more tenacious fighter will be victorious. The initial advantage is definitely gained by the opponent who is aware of the situation and jumps into the enemy airhead deliberately. If, in addition, he is supported from the outside by a concentrated thrust on the ground, it is quite likely that he will succeed in achieving a complete victory. The only question is whether, in the case of a large scale airborne operation which definitely presupposes the air superiority of the attacker, the defender will be in any position to carry out an air landing. At night this might be conceivable. In any event, such a counter-jump likewise requires preparations and is therefore possible only if the attacker lands in an area where the defender has taken such preparatory measures.

## Section VII.
## AN APPRAISAL OF ALLIED AIR LANDINGS

During a war, the success of one side and the failure of the other are interrelated. In general, the success of the defender's measures can best be judged by the degree to which the attacker, as the active party, has been able to realize his goal. From this point of view the three major Allied airborne operations during 1944-45 will be briefly evaluated.

The Allied air landings in Normandy in June 1944 were carried out in close tactical collaboration with the amphibious operations. The Germans expected the air landings to take place farther inland, and to be aimed at more strategic objectives. Defensive measures were taken accordingly. The choice of landing areas for the over-all operations came as a surprise and, consequently, the defensive front was such that in comparison with other areas it was inadequately fortified and was held by weak German forces. The majority of the German reserve was committed elsewhere and was only reluctantly released for action.

Passive defense measures taken by the Germans did not influence the progress of the Allied airborne operations to any large extent. The first air landing, owing to an error in orientation, was dispersed far beyond the originally planned area. This caused the dissipation of initial German counter-measures. Isolated German successes were not able to prevent the over-all success of the air landing. Besides, since the drop zones covered a large area, it was difficult for the German command to quickly gain an accurate picture of the situation. This resulted in the erroneous commitment of the reserves and also had an adverse effect on the morale of the German troops. Because of the unmistakable air superiority of the enemy, it was impossible for the German counter-measures to be executed rapidly enough. The German counter-attacks were able to narrow the landing areas temporarily and to limited extent; they succeeded in preventing the troops which had landed from immediately taking the offensive. They also succeeded in temporarily placing the Allied airborne troops in critical situations.

The German reserves were almost completely tied down by the air landings, making it impossible to launch effective counter-attacks against the amphibious assault. Consequently, the attackers were able to gain a foothold on the coast and, within a short time, to establish contact with the airborne elements. The tactical objective of establishing a bridgehead as thus accomplished despite German counter-measures.

The significant fact is that the air landings made it possible to substantially increase the number of forces which had been brought to the mainland during the first phase, thus augmenting the purely numerical superiority of the attacker over the defender.

It is open to question whether air landings with distinct concentration of forces on tactical objectives would have caused a more rapid collapse of the German over-all defense. Of course, the landings on the beaches would then have been more difficult. It also might have been possible to unify the German counter-measures against the invasion more effectively. The chances for greater victory would have involved a greater risk.

The air landings at Eindhoven, Nijmegen, and Arnhem in September 1944 were directed at breaking up the German front and paving the way for the British troops to reach the northern flank of the Ruhr area via the Meuse, the Waal, and the lower Rhine Rivers. The plan of attack offered the best chances of a major strategic victory. The operations also differed greatly from the Normandy landing in that they occurred during mobile warfare. Consequently, the Germans were unable to take defensive measures to the extent possible under conditions of position warfare. On the basis of intelligence reports, the Germans had anticipated enemy airborne operations. Furthermore, the commanders in the near-by home defense zones (Wehrkreis VI and Luftgau VI), as well as those in Holland, had made arrangements well in advance in order to be able to quickly form motorized auxiliary forces (so-called alert units) from home defense troops and occupation forces. These measures proved very effective, although the fighting strength of the alert units was necessarily limited.

In conformity with German principles, the air landings were attacked as soon as they were recognized. Two factors proved particularly helpful for the Germans. First, the air landing was not accompanied by any major attack by the Allied ground forces, but was supported only by a thrust on a narrow front launched by relatively weak armored spearheads, and was not followed by a heavier attack until the next day; secondly, the weather changed. Consequently, as early as the next day, the reinforcement and resupply of the airheads was considerably hampered and nearly ceased altogether for several days. At the same time the operations of the Allied air force against the German counter-measures, which in Normandy had caused so much damage, were greatly curtailed for some days.

The German counter-attacks against the two southern airheads in the area of Eindhoven and south of Nijmegen neither managed to crush them completely nor prevented their joining forces with the advancing ground elements. However, the Germans repeatedly succeeded in causing critical situations which delayed the advance of the Allied ground forces. Specifically, they managed to hold the bridge at Nijmegen for another four days, thus preventing the enemy from establishing contact with the northernmost airheads at Arnhem.

At Arnhem, in the meantime, the counter-attacks conducted under the unified command of Army Group B, whose operations staff was stationed there, had been successful. The two worn-out SS panzer divisions which by pure chance were still in the vicinity, and the above-mentioned alert units, whose fighting strength was negligible, were the only troops available at the time. Nevertheless, the airheads of the 1st British Airborne Division was narrowed continually, until it was finally annihilated with the exception of small portions which escaped to the southern banks of the lower Rhine River.

The German tactics had proved successful. Although they had not been able to prevent a deep penetration by the enemy, the Germans had managed to dispel the great danger of a strategic break-through, such as the Allies had planned. It was another six months before the Allies were able to launch an attack across the Rhine.

The Allied airborne operation at the Rhine, north of Wesel in March 1945, involved two airborne divisions. They were dropped directly into the river defense zone, operating in closest tactical collaboration with the ground troops which were launching an attack across the river. This air landing had been prepared with the greatest attention to detail and was supported not only by a large scale commitment of air forces, totaling more than 8,500 combat planes in addition to over 2,000 transport planes, but also by the entire artillery on the western bank of the Rhine. It was practically a mass crossing of the river by air. The operation was a complete success for it was impossible to take any effective counter-measures. The German troops struck by the attack - worn-out divisions with limited fighting strength- defended their positions for only a short time before they were defeated. The only reserves available consisted of one training division whose troops had been widely dispersed to escape the incessant air attacks. This division was issued orders to launch a counter-attack, and one regimental group did temporarily achieve a minor success against the landed airborne troops. The rest of the division was not committed at all, because enemy low level planes completely wrecked all means of transportation.

## Section VIII. REFLECTIONS ON THE ABSENCE OF RUSSIAN AIR LANDINGS

It is surprising that during World War II the USSR did not attempt any large-scale airborne operations. Although Soviet Russia was the first country in the world which during peacetime had experimented with landing troops by air and had organized special units for this purpose, its wartime operations were confined to the commitment of small units which were dropped back of the German front for the purpose of supporting partisan activities and which had no direct tactical or strategic effect. The reasons can only be surmised and might have been any or all of the following:

In 1941, when the Soviet Union entered the war, the Red Air Force was far inferior to the Luftwaffe. It is likely that the awareness of this inferiority persisted until the final stages of the war.

The Russians are primarily at home on the ground and are not in their element on the water or in the air.

In 1941 the parachute troops that had existed during peacetime may well have been expended in ground combat during the initial emergency. Later on, other parachute units were activated. Perhaps they lacked the necessary confidence or were considered too valuable to be risked in operations for which success was not assured. It is also possible that during the last phase of the war such operations simply were no longer regarded as necessary.

Marshal Tukhachevski was the originator of the Soviet parachute forces and after his removal the driving force in this new and untried field may well have been lacking.

Be that as it may, the fact that during World War II the Soviet armed forces did not carry out any large-scale airborne operations, such as were carried out by the Germans in Crete and by the Allies in Holland, should not lead to the false conclusion that the Soviet Union is not concerned with this problem or would fail to make use of this new arm during future military operations.

After finishing this study the author received additional information about an airborne operation carried out by the Russians late in the summer of 1943. Under cover of darkness, the Russians parachuted approximately three regiments into the area northwest of Kremenchug, about 25 miles behind the German front on the Dnepr. The exact date and place could not be given from memory. Only infantry forces without heavy weapons were dropped and they showed no initiative after the jump. Landing in small groups scattered over an area about 25 miles across, each group dug in on the spot, making no effort to contact other groups. Apparently they had no contact with their take-off base, and there were no simultaneous attacks by Russian ground forces across the Dnepr.

Within a few days the individual groups were mopped up with little difficulty at their separate landing places by German security formations and reserves. It was assumed that the Russian airborne troops would make their positions known to Russian airplanes by fires at night. The Germans therefore lit fires all along the river banks from Kremenchug to Kiev during the night following the jump. The Russians parachuted no further troops nor did they drop any supplies after the night of the landing. It is unknown whether a follow-up was intended or if it did not take place because of the uncertainty of the location of the landed forces brought about by the German deceptive measures.

The whole enterprise left the impression of inadequate preparation. Inadequate reconnaissance, mistakes in navigation during the approach and jump, lack of contact among the individual groups and between them and their base, as well as the complete passivity of the parachuted troops were the main deficiencies. The enterprise must be considered a complete failure. This may be why it remained so obscure that all German officers interviewed in connection with the original study, including General Student, General Blumentritt, and General Meindl (all officers with a comprehensive knowledge in this field), unanimously and independently stated that no large-scale airborne operations had been carried out by the Russians during World War II. As a result of investigation it was confirmed by a second informant that this Russian airborne operation actually took place at Kremenchug, but no further particulars could be procured.

Although this Russian airborne operation disclosed no new important experience in opposing airborne attacks, it seems appropriate to mention it if only for its singularity. Its complete failure may be a further reason, in addition to those mentioned above, for the absence of other large-scale Russian airborne operations in the course of the war. The impression prevails that tactically and technically the Russians could not meet the requirements of such an enterprise. Further reasons may be that the Russian soldier as a rule is not a good individual fighter but prefers to fight in mass formations, and that the junior Russian commanders lacked initiative and aggressiveness, two qualities that are basic requirements in a parachute officer.

The main effort of the Russian paratroopers during the war was without doubt in partisan warfare, an old method of combat that has always been favored by the Russians. In this field parachuting was widely exploited. However, this is a special subject having nothing to do with tactical airborne operations, and is therefore outside the province of this study.

# CHAPTER 3

# CONCLUSIONS

## Section I. EVALUATION OF PAST AIRBORNE EXPERIENCE

In spite of rockets and atom bombs, it is still the possession of the land, the conquest of enemy territory, that will decide the issue in a war. The possession of the land is the visible sign of victory, and its occupation is a guarantee of the exercise of complete control The occupying power definitely deprives the enemy of all chances of exploiting the territory with regard to natural resources, raw materials, industries, population, air bases, etc., while the occupier is able to utilize these for his own benefit and in the end force the enemy to surrender. The prerequisite, however, for the capture, the occupation, and the holding of a territory is the elimination of the enemy fighting forces which can defend the country and dispute its possession.

For a long time the most effective means of eliminating the enemy fighting forces seemed to be the method of envelopment, which is stressed particularly in the German theory of the art of war. An envelopment is directed at the enemy's weakest spot and cuts him off from his rear communications. During World War I the increasing effectiveness of weapons and the expansion of armies lessened the chances for large-scale envelopments and led to extended front lines with flanks anchored on impregnable points. The tactics of envelopment were replaced by the break-through, which during World War II was the objective of the mobile and combat-efficient panzer formations.

Airborne operations, carried out for the first time during World War II, point to a new trend. An air landing behind the enemy front is, after all, nothing but an envelopment by air, an envelopment executed in the third dimension. Herein lies its significance and an indication of the role it will play in future wars.

World War II has shown that airborne operations are practicable; furthermore, the results have proved that air landings are not one-time measures which owe their effectiveness exclusively to the element of surprise and then can no longer be applied. On the contrary, the events of World War II have demonstrated that it is extremely difficult for a defender to prevent or render ineffectual any airborne operations which are carried out with superior forces.

The airborne operations carried out during World War II still represent in every respect purely tactical measures taken in closest cooperation with the ground forces. Strategic concepts rarely entered into the picture. Even the capture of an island represented an individual action of strictly limited scope.

The continued technical improvement of all types of aircraft since the end of the war with regard to speed, range, and carrying capacity makes it appear quite possible that the scope of airborne operations will also increase in proportion to the number of forces and weapons which can be employed. Even today, it is probably no longer utopian to think of air landings as large-scale envelopments or even, beyond that, as outflanking movements in the third dimension, which will no longer merely aim at attacking the enemy's position from the rear, but will force him to relinquish his position in order to form an inverted front against the attacking forces that have landed far behind his lines.

For the most part, such considerations are limited by technical factors. This study cannot determine what these limitations are and how they apply to the present or the future, if only for the reason that the author lacks the necessary technical information. Besides, at the present rapid rate of technical progress, today's daydreams may be accomplished facts by tomorrow. This report, therefore, merely represents an analysis of some of the problems involved in airborne operations and a general evaluation of the resulting possibilities.

# Section II.
# LIMITATIONS OF AIRBORNE OPERATIONS

First of all, it should be remembered that airborne operations are governed by the same strategic and tactical principles that apply to any envelopment or flanking movement. A correct evaluation of the terrain and the time element, the ratio of friendly and enemy forces as well as the proper depth of attack in proportion to the available troops, the concentration of forces in a main effort and arrangements for containing the enemy at other points, the elements of surprise and deception-all have to be weighed and taken into account just as carefully as in ground operations. Consequently, they do not have to be discussed in further detail at this point.

The new element in airborne operations is the peculiarity of the approach via the third dimension, that is, by air. The accompanying difficulties as well as advantages should therefore be analyzed with particular care and must be taken into account in an evaluation of the above-mentioned factors.

In the main, this new method of attack by air gives rise to the following difficulties:

1.  The forces employed for air landings are highly vulnerable while they are on the approach route. This necessitates control of the air along the entire route, from the take-off points up to and including the landing area. Apart from other factors, the geographic limits of the area in which the attacker enjoys air supremacy determine the depth of a large-scale airborne operation.

2.  An air landing, more so than any operation on the ground, is a thrust into unknown territory. The conventional means of reconnaissance and sources of information offer inadequate results and require a great deal of time. From the moment the airborne troops land, they face surprises against which they are not protected by advance reconnaissance and security measures and from which they are no longer able to escape.

Consequently, every airborne operation involves a greater risk than ordinary ground combat, requires more time for preparation, and entails a distinct moment of weakness during the first phase of landing.

3. After the initial landing the fighting strength and mobility of airborne forces depend on their chances for resupply by air. It will no doubt be possible to improve the purely technical facilities available for this purpose. In this respect the military planners need not be afraid of asking too much from the men who are responsible for research and development. The really decisive factor is whether the military situation in the air permits the air transport of supplies. Just how far the attacker's air supremacy can be extended, not only in space but also in time, is a fundamentally important question. Another vital consideration is the time interval until contact with friendly ground troops can and must be established. The proper evaluation of these possibilities will always be the determining factor for the extent and scope of airborne operations and hence for the selection of suitable objectives as well. These difficulties are not insurmountable. They will be overcome by technical progress, organization and training of the forces, and proper tactical and strategic commitment, always of course within reasonable limits and with the necessary prerequisites.

4. However, there is one unalterable difficulty-the inflexibility of an airborne operation at the time of execution. Once the plan has been decided upon and the operation has been set into motion, the entire action necessarily has to unfold according to schedule. The only control the high command can still exercise is through the commitment of its reserves. The initiative exercised by intermediate and lower echelons, which in ordinary ground combat assures flexibility of adjustment to the existing situation and which in the German Army was particularly stressed as a vital combat

requirement, is largely eliminated during airborne operations. It cannot begin to take effect until an attack is launched from the captured airhead. Only in part can these deficiencies be offset by careful and detailed preparations, which take time, and by committing even greater quantities of troops and materiel, which again proves that airborne warfare is a "rich man's" weapon.

*[Field Marshal Kesselring's comments on the inflexibility of airborne operations:*

*I do not agree that airborne operations are absolutely tied to a fixed schedule and are therefore too rigid in their execution. Naturally, an airborne operation executed according to plan will be assured the greatest probability of success. Should the situation require a sweeping change in plans, however, this can be carried out by signal communications from ground to air and between the flying formations. This will require the preparation of alternate plans and intensive training of the units. Formations on the approach flight can be recalled or can be ordered to land at previously designated alternate fields. This is less complicated in the case of later serials. In my opinion such changes can be carried out more easily in the air than on the ground. In land warfare, once large formations are committed in a certain direction toward a definite objective, major and minor changes involve equal difficulties. There is no reason why this should be any different in an airborne operation.]*

## Section III.
## ADVANTAGES OF AIRBORNE OPERATIONS

Despite the cost in men and materiel, airborne operations offer such outstanding advantages that no future belligerent with the necessary means at his disposal can be expected to forego using this combat method. The following are the main advantages:

The airborne operation makes it possible for the attacker to carry out a vertical envelopment or to outflank front lines or lines

*A welcome cigarette calms the nerves during the fighting on the Italian front.*

with protected flanks; it also enables him to surmount terrain obstacles which interfere with the movements of ground troops, such as wide rivers, channels, mountains, and deserts.

The airborne operation can be launched from the depth of the attacker's zone. It develops with extraordinary speed and offers remarkable opportunities for surprise attacks, with regard to time and place, and thus forestalls any counter-measures by the enemy.

The psychological effect of vertical envelopment is considerably greater than that produced by horizontal envelopment. It can affect the enemy command and troops solely by reason of its menace-the uncertainty of when and where an air landing might take place. The consequent effect on the population of the country, either positive or negative as the case may be, should also not be underestimated.

## Section IV. REQUIREMENTS FOR SUCCESS

An armed force desiring to overcome the difficulties which arise from the use of airborne operations and seeking to make the most of the advantages offered by such operations should, in consideration of the statements made so far, arrive at the following conclusions:

The attacker's air force should be so strong that even at the beginning of the war it will either be wholly superior to the enemy, or, in fighting the enemy air force, will seriously weaken that force and thus pave the way for mastery of the air with regard to time and space.

It is necessary to have available a highly qualified specialized force for the execution of airborne operations. Air landings require tough fighters eager for action, an intensive and diversified training, the best kind of equipment, and ample air-transport space. It is advisable to recruit this specialized force from volunteers. Men who have been taken from the militia or conscript army and have received only brief training, might require an extended tour of active duty. Above all, however, this force should be activated in peacetime, not in cadres only but in full strength, since such a specialized force cannot be organized quickly. These requirements again demonstrate that airborne operations will always be something which only the "rich man" can afford.

Any planning for airborne operations on a large scale should include preparations for the movement by air of large ground unit (divisions) to permit the prompt reinforcement of airborne troops after their initial landing. The necessary adjustments with regard to equipment and organization must be carefully considered and applied, and specialized gear must be at hand.

It should be realized that an airborne operation is as rapid in its execution as it is time consuming in its preparation and affords neither much freedom of maneuver nor a great deal of flexibility; it must be prepared well in advance. Once it has been set into motion, its direction and objective can no longer be changed. Even in peace-time it is therefore necessary to draw up blueprints for certain conceivable airborne operations, blueprints which are to be carefully modified on the basis of current information obtained in the course of actual hostilities. If this work has been done, the time required for preparation in each individual case can be considerably reduced. Only through foresighted preparatory work covering several likely situations is it at all possible to achieve a limited degree of flexibility in the execution of airborne operations.

Finally, it should also be mentioned that air landings, even more than any other operations, are dependent on the weather. The more territory an airborne operation is supposed to cover, the greater will be the need for a long-range weather forecast system, which even during peacetime will have to be set up with an eye to functioning under such wartime limitations as the absence of weather data from enemy countries.

## Section V. ANTI-AIRBORNE DEFENSE

With regard to defense measures against airborne operations, the following conclusions may be drawn from this study:

The best method of defense is and always will be a strong air force.

The next requirement is a well-organized observation (radar) and warning system; it is essential to succeed in setting up this network quickly, even in a war of movement, and to adapt it to the fluctuating situations.

Local defense measures and preparations for all-around defense are increasingly important for rear elements. In addition, it will be necessary to establish clearly who, in the rear areas, will be in command of all forces which have to be committed in case of enemy air landings, and who will be responsible-for making the necessary arrangements to this effect.

In an era of constantly growing possibilities for operations far behind the front lines, the need for prompt and forceful action against hostile air landings will eventually force any belligerent to scatter his strategic reserves over the whole of his communications zone, and even parts of the zone of the interior; he may also be compelled to hold large forces in readiness for the express purpose of defending his rear areas against long-range enemy airborne operations.

## Section VI. FUTURE POSSIBILITIES

Future wars will offer far-reaching possibilities for the employment of airborne operations. The selection and scope of the objectives will always depend on the available forces (air force, airborne troops) and consequently will be a question of war potential. But the employment of airborne operations as a weapon in future wars also will depend on an early decision to make use of it, because air landings cannot be improvised, either in obtaining the necessary forces or in the technical aspects of the operation itself.

At the beginning of World War II, the strategic employment of armor completely changed the concepts of warfare carried over from World War I; it is quite conceivable that, at the beginning of a future war, the employment of large airborne units will play a similar role.

# NOTES ON GERMAN AIRBORNE OPERATIONS

## *By Col. Freiherr von der Heydte*

## Section I. EQUIPMENT OF GERMAN PARACHUTE TROOPS

During the war, the weapons and equipment of German parachute troops did not differ essentially from those of the infantry. The paratroop automatic rifle, which used standard ammunition, was the only special type of small arms developed. It was adopted because the automatic rifle of the infantry did not use standard ammunition. In any paratroop operation the most harassing problem was the method of carrying ammunition. Since the rifle was attached to the man while jumping, the weapons containers, most of which after 1942 were transportable, became available for carrying ammunition. In 1944 a so-called ammunition vest for each man was introduced in some parachute units and proved successful.

Immediately after the Crete operation the paratroops had requested the construction of special midget tanks (Lilliputpanzer), which could be carried along on airborne operations, as well as special light weight portable antitank guns. Experiments were begun in 1942 on a two-man tank which could be transported in a large troop-carrying glider and which because of its shape was called a "turtle." Because of difficulties in the armament production program, the experiments were discontinued toward the end of 1942 before it was possible to form a definite opinion on the usefulness of the model. In any case, it seems to have met the Army's three requirements of low silhouette, high speed, and great cross-country mobility as fully

*A member of the XI Fliegerkorps standing with ammunition belt and shouldered MG 42 machine gun in Russia.*

as possible.

In 1942 the paratroops were given a 48-mm./42-mm. antitank gun with tapered bore and solid projectile as a special weapon for antitank fighting instead of the impractical 37-mm. antitank gun, which was difficult to transport. The gun did not prove especially successful in Africa against the heavy British tanks and its production was discontinued in 1943. At the same time the so-called Panzerwurfmine (magnetic antitank hand grenade) was introduced as a special weapon for fighting tanks at close range, but it was soon replaced by the Panzerfaust (recoilless antitank grenade and launcher, both expendable). In autumn 1944 the German engineer Schardien was working on a new close-range antitank device for airborne use which would have been easier to transport than the Panzerfaust; he was probably unable to complete his experiments.

Some of the paratroop units used the so-called Einstoss-flammenwerfer (one-thrust flame thrower) of the SS, which was considerably better adapted to paratroop use than the Army flame thrower.

The greatest headache for the German paratroop command

was the lack of artillery in support of infantry fighting. The German paratroops were equipped with the excellent 75-mm. and 105-mm. airborne recoilless guns; both had short barrels and carriages made of light metal alloy. In suitable terrain the 75-mm. gun could be easily drawn by two men, and its elevation was the same as that of the 37-mm. antitank gun of the Army. The maximum range was 3,850 yards for the 75-mm. gun and 9,000 yards for the 105-mm. gun. Both had the following disadvantages:

a.  A large amount of smoke and fumes was generated, and the flash toward the rear was visible at night for a great distance.

b.  They could be used only as flat-trajectory weapons. Attempts to use the airborne recoilless guns as high-angle weapons were not satisfactory. Moreover, in an airborne operation it was seldom possible to carry along the necessary amount of ammunition or have it brought up later. Thus, as a rule, only important point targets could be attacked with single rounds, generally from an exposed fighting position.

Besides these weapons, 150-mm. rocket projectiles were used in the Crete operation. They were fired from wooden carrying crates, which also served as aerial delivery containers. These rockets did not prove successful; because of their high degree of dispersion they were suitable only for use against area targets and in salvo fire. However, the quantity of projectiles needed for such a purpose could not be transported on an airborne operation, and a JU-52 (German troop carrier) could carry and drop only four projectiles at a time.

The parachute troops were generally forced to rely on Army signal equipment which, to be sure, was available to them in far greater quantities than it was to any other units. The "Dora" and "Friedrich" radio sets proved very successful in German air landing operations. Ever since 1942 the troops had repeatedly requested in addition a small, portable short-range radio set for communicating between companies, but no such set was introduced. Several units, therefore, made use of captured American equipment. For the projected Malta operation of one parachute battalion, the engineering firm of Siemens-Halske supplied a portable radio set for maintaining contact with the base. It had a definite range of 180 miles, could be operated without interruption for six hours, and could easily be carried by one man.

Carrier pigeons and messenger dogs proved very successful in airborne operations; the former for communicating with the base, the latter for communication within the company or from company to battalion. The dogs, equipped with a parachute that was automatically disconnected from the harness after landing, generally jumped very willingly and without accidents. In 1942 a signal cartridge, protected against misuse by the enemy by a special contrivance, was introduced on an experimental basis. However, the experiment was very soon discontinued.

## Section II. GERMAN EMPLOYMENT OF TROOP-CARRIER UNITS

In Holland in 1940, the Germans came to realize the disadvantage of the parachute commander's inability to exercise any direct authority over the troop-carrier units; the two were coordinated, but neither was subordinate to the other. Consequently, before carrying out the Crete operation the troop-carrier units were incorporated into the parachute corps, of which they constituted an integral part under a special Luftwaffe officer (Fliegerfuehrer). This arrangement did not last long. The operations in Russia and North Africa required the concentration of all air transport services directly under the commander in chief of the Luftwaffe to assure the prompt execution of any air transport operations which might become necessary, and only in the rarest cases did this involve carrying paratroops. As a result the training of troop-carrier units was also reorganized. The pilots were then trained to fly in "main bodies" (Pulk) or in a "stream of bombers" (Bomberstrom), that is, in irregular formations which were always three dimensional. However, it is impossible to drop parachutists from the Pulk or Bomberstrom formations; dropping parachutists requires a regular flight in formation at a uniform altitude, that is, a two-dimensional flight. The close flight order of the conventional heavy bomber formation, with its effective cross fire on all sides, is desirable for approach flights across hostile territory. It provides defense against enemy fighter planes and can be maintained until shortly before the parachute or airplane landings. If there is a probability of strong anti-aircraft fire, the plane-to-plane and group-to-group spacing will have to be increased. For such tactics, intensive training of the troop-carrier pilots will be necessary, especially in the proper deployment preparatory to parachute drops.

Losses during the attack on Leros in the autumn of 1943 are said to have occurred mainly because the troop carriers did not fly in regular formation and at the same altitude; during the air landing in the Ardennes in December 1944 it proved a fatal mistake that the troop-carrier units were no longer accustomed to flying in regular formation. The experience gained both at Leros and in the Ardennes has shown that it is essential for a troop-carrier unit which is to drop parachutists to be trained to do this work, since a good part of the success of an airborne operation depends on flying in regular close formation at the same altitude. It is obvious that the necessary training in formation flying is best achieved if the troop-carrier units are subordinated to the command of airborne troops from the very first. Up to the end of the war the German paratroop command continued to demand that it be given permanent control over the troop-carrier units, but this demand remained unfulfilled. That the troop-carrier units must be subordinate to the airborne command at least for the duration of an operation is clear to everyone. The fallacy of letting non-specialists make decisions in such matters was demonstrated in the less than brilliant direction of the Leros operation by a naval officer (the Commanding Admiral, Aegean). Likewise the Ardennes operation, which was prepared by an Air officer (the Air Force Commander, West), and carried out by an Army officer (the Commanding General, Sixth SS Panzer Army); one knew as little about an airborne operation and its difficulties as did the other.

Although the problem of cooperation between the airborne command and the command of the troop-carrier units was solved at least temporarily during the Crete operation, the cooperation, or lack of it, between the individual airborne unit and the individual troop-carrier squadron continued to be the greatest cause of complaint by the airborne troops during the entire war. At best, the individual airborne battalion commander became personally acquainted with the commander of the transport group which flew his battalion only 2 or 3 days before the operation; as a rule, the individual soldier did not establish any contact with the flying crew of the machine which had to transport him. There was no mutual understanding of peculiarities, capabilities, and shortcomings. The 2d Battalion of the 1st Paratroop Regiment was almost completely annihilated in Crete because the battalion commander of the airborne troops greatly overestimated the flying ability of the troop-carrier unit which was to carry his men, whereas the commander of the troop-carrier force, on the other hand, did not understand the extremely elaborate plan of attack of the airborne commander, who was a complete stranger to him. In former times one would not require a cavalry regiment to carry out an attack when its men had only been given a short course in riding but had not been issued any horses until the night before the attack.

Next to the pilot, the most important man in the flying crew was the airborne combat observer, or, as the troops called him, the jump-master (Absetzer), that is, the man who gave the signal to jump. The jump-master should be an extremely well-trained observer and bombardier. In the German airborne forces he was just the opposite. The jump-masters were not taken from the flying personnel of the Luftwaffe but from the airborne troops; from time to time, the various parachute units had to release one or two men for training as jump-masters, and with the inherent selfishness of any unit they naturally did not release their best men but rather their worst, who for some reason or other could no longer be used as paratroopers. If this reason was a combat injury, the men might still have served their purpose, but more often than not the reason was lack of personal courage or intelligence. The jump-masters selected in this negative manner were trained at a jump-masters' school by instructors who had been detailed from the flying personnel of the Luftwaffe. The Luftwaffe did not release its best instructors for this purpose. After this deficient training the jump-master waited in some troop-carrier unit, like the fifth wheel on a wagon, until he was needed for an airborne operation, meanwhile forgetting what little he had learned at the school. For, like bombing or firing a weapon, dropping paratroops is a matter of practice, of constant uninterrupted practice. The German jump-masters were completely lacking in this practice. In almost every airborne operation the consequences were disastrous. During the Crete operation at least one platoon of each battalion was landed incorrectly; at Maleme entire companies were dropped into the sea because the jump-masters- out of fear, as the paratroopers afterwards claimed-had given the signal too early; during the Ardennes operation one company was dropped on the Rhine north of Bonn instead of south of Eupen, and the majority of the signal platoon of that company was dropped south of Monschau directly in front of the German lines.

Only on two occasions, the operation near Eben Emael in 1940 and the projected operation of dive-gliders against Malta in 1942, were paratroopers and troop-carrier units brought together for orientation and joint training for a considerable period prior to the operations. In both cases cooperation was excellent.

## Section III. TECHNIQUE AND TACTICS OF AIRBORNE OPERATIONS

The German airborne forces carried out two kinds of airborne landingsthe parachute operation and the troop-carrying glider operation. After 1942, as a general principle, the parachute troops were trained in both kinds of airborne landings so that such units could be used at any time either in parachute or in glider operations, according to the tactical and terrain requirements.

The JU-52 and He-111 were available as troop-carrier planes. From the JU-12 the jump was made through the door, from the He-111 through a jump hatch. Jumping from the door proved more successful since the men were more willing to jump out of the door than through the hatch in the floor of the plane and because the landings were effected at considerably smaller time intervals. In a well-trained unit 13 men could leave the plane in not more than eight seconds. With the planes moving at a speed of 100 to 120 miles per hour and at an altitude of about 330 feet (100 meters), there would be a distance of about 25 yards between men immediately after landing; that is, the group reached the ground in a fairly compact formation and could be immediately assembled by the unit commander if the terrain offered a reasonable degree of visibility.

The jumping altitude was generally a little more than 330 feet. As commander of the instruction battalion, the author carried out tests at lower jump altitudes; at a jump altitude of 200 feet, the lowest that was reached, casualties through jumping injuries rose to an average of 20 percent. As soon as the jumping altitude was raised much in excess of 330 feet, the ground dispersion of the group increased. According to experience gained in the instruction battalion, a jumping altitude of about 670 feet resulted in an average dispersion of a group of 13 men amounting to 900 yards in depth and over 200 yards in width, about twice the average dispersion attained with a jumping altitude of 330 feet.

Jump casualties as well as dispersion depended largely on the velocity of surface wind, the determining of which was, or should have been, one of the most important special tasks of the combat reconnaissance directly preceding any landing operation. In general, German paratroops were only able to jump with a surface wind not over 14 miles per hour. Operations with a surface wind of greater velocity resulted in many jump casualties and often delayed the assembly of the landed troops for hours. The relatively large losses from jump casualties during the airborne operation against the island of Leros in the autumn of 1943 must be attributed entirely to the high surface wind. During the airborne operation in the Ardennes in December 1944 a surface wind of 36 miles per hour caused heavy casualties. Of the elements of one airborne unit which could still be assembled after the jump, more than 10 percent were injured in jumping, which did not, however, prevent most of them from taking part in the fighting a few hours later.

The German parachute fell short of requirements. It caused an excessive swinging motion in gusty weather, it was hard to control, and too much time was required to get out of the harness. Too much importance was probably attached to safety in jumping and too little to suitability for combat operations. The casualties which were sustained from enemy action because the soldier was unable to free himself from his harness quickly enough were far greater than the casualties which might have been caused by carelessness in opening the single fastening harness release in the air. During the Ardennes operation I myself made an experimental jump with a captured Russian triangular parachute which despite strong gusts and a surface wind of 36 miles per hour brought me to earth with almost no oscillation.

At the time, I still had my left arm in a temporary splint. In that wind it would have been impossible to jump with a German parachute when one's arm was in a splint.

Too much importance was attached to the rigging of parachutes; valuable training time and time prior to an operation was lost because every man had to rig his own parachute. In my regiment I made the experiment of introducing a parachute maintenance platoon which rigged the parachutes for the entire regiment. The results were very good. Jumping experiments with unrigged parachutes have shown that in an emergency it is sufficient to make two air-resistance folds (Luftschlagfalten) and that much of the complicated packing procedure was mere fussiness.

Since heavy casualties had been sustained in Crete because the paratroopers could not reach their weapon containers or because they had to leave cover in order to unpack the containers, after 1942 regular training was given in jumping with the weapons attached to the soldier. This proved very successful. The soldier carried any one of the following items on his person: pistol, submachine gun, rifle, light machine gun, boxes of ammunition for machine guns and medium mortars, machine gun carriage, or short entrenching tool. In addition, each of the following items of equipment was dropped successfully by auxiliary parachute attached to a soldier: medium mortar barrel, medium mortar base plate, and "Dora" and "Friedrich" radio set.

At first the German airborne troops placed too much emphasis on the nature of the terrain at the drop point. Practical experiences during the war showed that well-trained troops can make combat jumps anywhere, except in terrain without cover where enemy fire is likely to engage the paratroops immediately after landing. Moreover, rocky terrain is particularly unfavorable. A landing in woods presents no difficulties in jumping technique, although it makes assembly very difficult after the jump. During training, German paratroopers frequently jumped into wooded areas, but in combat only once-in the Ardennes operation in 1944. It is also possible to land among groups of houses, that is, on roofs. Of course, this requires special training and equipment. The paratrooper must be able to cling to the roof with the aid of grappling hooks and quickly cut an opening in the roof so that he can make his way into the house.

Regular training in night jumping first began in 1942 and soon produced good results. After 1943 the requirements for the award of the paratrooper's insignia after the completion of training included at least one jump at night. In combat, night jumps were made by the Germans on only one occasion, during the Ardennes operation. Night jumping presented two main difficulties-locating the drop point, and establishing contact after jumping. For locating the drop point which had to be reached accurately by every airplane within a few hundred yards, the radio-control procedure customary in night bombing operations was not satisfactory since it was too inaccurate and led to many errors. In practice, therefore, the Germans made use of two other procedures to supplement rather than replace radio control: a technical radio device, the so-called radio buoy (Funkboje) and the incendiary-bomb field (Brandbombenfeld). The radio buoy was a shockproof, short-range radio transmitter packed in an aerial delivery container, which was released over the drop zone by a pathfinder plane flying ahead of the troop carrier unit and then automatically gave each troop carrier the signal for dropping as soon as the aircraft had flown to within a certain area. The experiments with the radio buoy, which were carried out after 1943, had not yet been concluded to complete satisfaction by the end of the war. Therefore, during the Ardennes operation the author made use of the simpler method, the incendiary-bomb field. Two fields of incendiary bombs were laid out on the ground about one mile apart by a pathfinder plane of the troop-carrier unit, and the landing unit was to be dropped halfway between these two incendiary-bomb fields. This was not successful in the Ardennes operation, not because of any defects in the procedure but rather because of the strong American ground defenses and the unbelievably bad training of the flying personnel of the two troop carrier units engaged in the mission. Cooperation with pathfinders in night jumping requires the most accurate timing. Because of incorrect wind data, the pathfinders in the Ardennes operation arrived at the drop zone almost a quarter of an hour too early. In this way not only was the American air defense warned in advance, but the last transport planes were no longer guided and had to drop their men blindly.

In order to establish contact on the ground after a night jump the Germans generally used acoustical signals, such as bird calls and croaking of frogs, in preference to optical communication. Radio was used only to establish contact between company and company and between company and battalion. In the summer of 1942 experiments were made with jumps in bad weather and in fog, but without satisfactory results.

The Germans distinguished between two kinds of operation with troop carrying gliders-gliding flight and diving flight. Great results were expected of the latter in particular. The same craft were used for both operations, either the small DFS which could carry 10 men with light equipment or the larger Go, a glider with a double tail assembly which could carry a load equivalent to one German 75-mm. antitank gun, including a two-man gun crew. The type of tow plane and method of towing were the same for both kinds of operation. The He-111 was mostly used as a towing aircraft. The JU-8 was best adapted for diving operations. In general, the cable tow was used to pull gliders; experiments with the rigid tow produced debatable results.

German gliders were specially equipped for diving operations. A "ribbon" parachute was provided as a diving brake. This consisted of several strips between which the air could pass.

*Dogged defence of the mountain positions in Italy.*

The glider pilot released this parachute by hand the moment the craft tipped downward. The take-off wheels were thrown off after the start, and the glider landed on a broad runner wrapped with barbed wire to increase the braking effect. This runner was directly behind the center of gravity of the glider. On some gliders designed for special types of operation there was a strong barbed hook, similar to an anchor, which dug into the ground during the landing. Finally, certain gliders were also provided with a braking rocket in the nose which could be automatically or manually ignited at the moment of landing and gave the landing machine a strong backward thrust. In some experiments a glider thus equipped was brought to a halt on a landing strip only 35 yards long.

An approach altitude of about 13,000 feet seemed particularly favorable for diving operations. The glider was released 20 miles before the objective and reached the diving point in a gliding flight. As a rule, the diving angle was 70 degrees to 80 degrees, the diving speed around 125 miles per hour, the altitude at which the pilot had to pull out of the dive about 800 feet. In diving, the glider could elude strong ground defense by spinning for a short time or by frequently changing its diving angle diving by steps (Treppensturz) as it was called. In training pilots for diving operations the greatest difficulty was experienced in teaching them to make an accurate spot landing, in which under certain circumstances even a few yards might be important, and to recognize the right moment for pulling out of the dive. To my knowledge, it was only once that the possibilities offered by dive-gliders were put to use in combat. In 1943 seven 75-mm. antitank guns were dropped into the citadel of Velikie Luki, which was surrounded by the Russians, by using Go's as dive-gliders. In connection with the projected paratroop operation against Malta in 1942, six hours before the parachute jump, a battalion under my command was supposed to land by means of dive-gliders among the British anti-aircraft positions on the south coast of the island and to eliminate the British ground defense. Over a period of months the Malta operation was prepared down to the smallest detail, and during that time the parachute troops practiced on mock-ups of these positions.

Toward the end of the war the German airborne forces clearly defined three methods of attacking an objective:

Jumping or landing on top of the objective;

Jumping or landing near the objective;

Jumping or landing at a distance from the objective.

According to German views, jumping or landing on top of the objective is the method primarily suited for attacking an objective which is relatively small and specially fortified against a ground attack. The Germans considered the troop-carrying dive-glider best suited for such an operation. Examples of landing on top of the objective are the capture of Fort Eben Emael north of Liege in 1940, the unsuccessful attack by elements of the airborne assault regiment (Sturmregiment) in gliders against British anti-aircraft positions near Khania on the island of Crete, and the jump by my combat group at the crossroads north of Mont Rigi, in the Eifel Mountains of western

Germany.

Jumping near the objective is the preferred method used for the capture of a bridge or an airfield. Here the general rule is that the men jump toward the objective from all sides, so that the target to be attacked lies, so to speak, in the center of a bell-shaped formation of descending troopers. Examples of jumping near the objective are the capture of the Moordijk bridges in 1940, the capture of the Waalhafen airfield near Rotterdam in 1940, and the capture of the Maleme airfield in Crete in 1941. While, in spite of the bravest fighting, the British did not succeed in capturing the Arnhem bridge from the air in 1944, this was probably in large part because they did not jump near their objective but at a considerable distance from it.

According to German views, jumping at a distance from the objective should be resorted to chiefly when the objective is so large that it can only be reduced by slow, systematic infantry attack; inch by inch, so to speak. Whereas in jumping near the objective it is a basic rule that the attack must be made from several sides, in jumping at a distance from the objective the attack on the ground must be launched on a deep, narrow front from one direction. An example of this method was presented in the attack by the 3d Parachute Regiment against the city of Khania on the island of Crete in 1941. To be sure, it is doubtful whether such an operation would today be carried out in the same manner. Since it has been determined that it is possible for paratroopers to attack buildings from the air, the best method of attack for the purpose of capturing a village might be a combination of jumping on top of the objective and jumping near the objective rather than the procedure used in Crete in 1941; evidently the easiest way to capture a village should be from within. To date, of course, no practical experiences are available on this subject.

As a result of their experiences the Germans distinguished between two ways of dropping a parachute force: landing all elements of a unit in the same area; landing all elements of a unit at the same time.

To accomplish the landing of all elements in the same area, the troop carriers approach the drop zone in a deep, narrow formation and all paratroopers jump into the same small area. For a battalion of 600 men, a landing area measuring about 900 yards in diameter and a landing time of about 30 minutes will be normal. According to German experience, this method of landing a unit is to be used especially at night, in jumping into woods or a village or other areas with low visibility, as well as in jumping at a distance from the objective. It was, for example, the mistake of the 3d Battalion of the 3d Parachute Regiment in Crete that it failed to choose this type of landing. Its heavy casualties can in part be attributed to this fact.

If all elements of a unit are to be landed at the same time, the troop carriers make their approach in wide formation to various drop zones situated close to each other and all paratroopers jump, as nearly as possible, at the same time. In such an operation, the landing area for a battalion of 600 men will usually measure at least 2,000 yards in diameter, with a landing time of less than 15 minutes. According to German experience, this method of landing a unit is to be especially recommended when jumping into terrain which offers little cover, as well as when jumping near the objective. In Crete, the 2d Battalion of the 1st Parachute Regiment made the mistake of landing at a number of widely separated small drop points at very long time intervals. As a result of the delay, the battalion was almost completely wiped out. It can be stated as a general rule that the larger the landing area, the less time should be spent in the dropping operation. Anyone who is careless with respect to time and space will be annihilated.

*[Field Marshall Kesselring's comments on the three methods of attacking an objective:*

*First method.-Airborne landings into an area which is*

*strongly defended against air attack can succeed only when there is absolute surprise. To be sure, the effect of weapons against parachutes in the air is generally overestimated. However, every landing harbors within itself a pronounced element of weakness which increases while troops are under the defensive fire of the enemy and which may lead to disaster during the very first moments of ground combat. The examples of Arnhem (1944) and Sicily (1943) speak only too eloquently for this; such examples will occur again and again. The attack against Fort Eben Emael can be considered as an example to the contrary. The study of this attack will enable one to recognize the possibilities and limitations of such operations.*

*Second method.-The prerequisites for a landing near the objective are correctly described. Such landings, however, should be planned so that they are not subject to the disadvantages which occur when jumping directly into the objective. When one has to reckon with strong anti-aircraft defenses, a success costing few casualties can generally be achieved only through surprise. Gliders are superior to parachutists because of their soundless approach.*

*Third method.-In large-scale operations it will be the rule to jump at a point some distance away from the objective. One should not belittle the advantage of landing, assembling, and organizing troops in an area which is out of danger! The factor of surprise is still retained to a greater or lesser extent according to the time of day or night, the weather conditions, and the terrain. A combination of landings into and near the objective may be advisable or necessary for tactical reasons or for deception, in order to scatter the enemy fire. The same purpose may be achieved by launching diversionary attacks when landing at some distance.]*

# GERMAN GLIDERS AND GLIDER-BORNE TROOPS

*Tactical and Technical Trends,*
*No. 14, December 17, 1942.*

### a. Organization of Gliderborne Troops

Gliderborne troops constitute one of the two German Air Force components operating under the Fliegerkorps XI. They are known as Sturmtruppen (assault troops) and are organized into a Sturmregiment. Although technically airlanding units, they must not be confused with the airlanding Army troops, which are infantry units.

Troops transported by gliders function in close conjunction with parachute troops and the Army airlanding detachments. In the general pattern of operations, they precede the parachute troops and, by their noiseless approach, utilize to the fullest the element of surprise. Their mission is to neutralize anti-aircraft and other defenses, and to disrupt all communication systems. They thus prepare the way for the parachutists who seize landing ground for the transports bearing the airlanding Army troops.

The assault regiment has a full strength of almost 2,000 men and is organized into 4 battalions having a total of 14 companies. Each of the first 3 battalions is broken down into a headquarters and signal unit, a heavy weapons company, and 3 rifle companies of 120 men each. A rifle company consists of 4 platoons, plus a headquarters and signal unit. Each platoon is divided into 3 sections of 10 men each. The fourth battalion includes a headquarters unit, a signal section, and 2 companies, infantry-gun and antitank.

The DFS-230 gliders, in which the assault troops are normally carried, are organized into a special air transport unit known as the Luftlandung Geschwader, the smallest operational unit of

*German glider - Gotha-242*

which is a Kette of 3 gliders. Each glider carries a complement of 10 men, which is a section of a platoon. Three flights or Ketten make up a Gruppe. The Geschwader is, therefore, composed of 4 Gruppen with a total of 192 gliders and can transport the entire Sturmregiment of approximately 2,000 men.

### b. Training

Glider pilots generally have had previous experience in civilian glider flying, although this does not qualify them for handling a freight-carrying glider. A 6 weeks' course in gliding is given in special training schools, particular stress being placed on spot landings. Training on large gliders is conducted within the glider unit itself. The troops carried by a glider are graduate parachutists; however, they do not normally wear parachutes in gliderborne operations. It is debatable that they parachuted from gliders over Crete as has been reported.

Training gliders are believed to fall within three classes according to wing span. The "A" class glider has a wing of high aspect ratio with 55- to 60-foot span and usually a very short nose. It is possible that some gliders in this class may be high-performance sailplanes. Gliders in the "B" or intermediary class, having a span of 35 to 50 feet, are probably the most widely used. The "C" class gliders, with a span of 33 to 35 feet, are believed to be used for primary training.

## c. Types of Gliders

Up to the present time the DFS-230 mentioned above is the only troop-carrying glider that has been identified as carrying assault troops during operations. The Gotha-242 (see following sketch), which has often been referred to as one of the principal troop transport gliders, is used almost entirely for carrying freight. This high-wing, dual-controlled glider is reported, however, to be capable of carrying 21 fully equipped men in addition to 2 pilots.

The Merseburg, which has been mentioned as a tank-carrying glider, has been estimated to accommodate 40 to 50 men, while the Goliath is veritably the giant glider that its name implies. This twin-fuselage glider is believed to have a wing span of 270 feet and a wing area of 7,500 square feet, and to carry 17 to 20 tons or 140 fully equipped men, 70 in each fuselage. These gliders are in a more or less experimental stage and are therefore not considered for the purpose of this discussion as a part of the Geschwader organization.

The DFS-230 used in the Cretan campaign is a high-wing monoplane with a wing span of 71 feet 5 inches and a length of approximately 36 feet. It has fabric-covered wings and a fuselage of steel tubular construction. The wheels can be jettisoned after the take-off, and a landing is effected on a central skid. The empty weight of this glider, fixed equipment included, is approximately 2,200 pounds, and the (tare) fully loaded weight 4,600 pounds. Weight varies according to the assignment involved; a useful load is probably about 2,400 pounds.

This glider will carry nine fully equipped men and one pilot. Seats are arranged in a single line on a boom running along the center of the fuselage, six facing forward and four backward. The rear seats are detachable in case more space is needed for freight. A 24-volt storage battery installed in the nose of the glider furnishes power for navigation, cabin, and landing lights. A fixed light machine gun (LMG-34) is believed to be attached

*A Fallschirmjäger collects equipment from a DFS 230 glider used in the assault on Crete, May 1941.*

externally to the starboard side of the fuselage and fired by the man in the seat behind the pilot. Instruments on the panel of the DFS- 230 include altimeter, compass, and airspeed, rate-of-climb, and turn-and-bank indicators.

The DFS-230 is ordinarily towed by a Ju-52 aircraft, which normally flies empty. Towing planes usually fly in a Kette; but when two or three gliders are towed, each is attached directly to the tug in V-formation. The glider is towed by means of a rope or a steel cable attached to a hook in the tail of the aircraft and fitted with a quick-release mechanism. The length of the towing line depends on the airfield space available; the longer the rope the easier the handling. A multiple tug arrangement probably would be necessary to tow a glider the size of the Goliath or the Merseburg. Three or four Me-110's or three Ju-52's might give a reasonable performance, although this would be a difficult operation.

### d. Glider Operations

Gliders do not require large landing areas, runways being desirable but not essential. The landing run of a DFS-230 is said to have been shortened by wrapping barbed wire around the skids. Flaps are used to steepen the angle of the glide. In case of Me-110's being used as tugs, rocket-assisted take-off may be necessary when using airdromes with runways less than 2,000 feet.

The range of operations of a glider is obviously dependent on the range of the towing aircraft. The total range for the Ju-52 with 530 gallons of fuel in still-air conditions when towing one DFS-230 is about 780 miles, or 600 miles for three gliders. This will allow an approximate radius of action of 250 miles. With extra fuel a Ju-52 is reported to be able to tow a DFS-230 more than 1,000 miles.

The distances which gliders can cover after the release vary according to altitude of release, direction and force of wind relative to line of flight, navigation errors, and evasive action. The gliding distance for the DFS-230 has been calculated in the ratio of 1 to 16 in still air, i.e. for every foot of descent, the glider theoretically covers 16 feet measured horizontally. In Crete, gliders are believed to have been released at not more than 2 to 5 miles from shore and at altitudes not more than 5,000 feet, permitting a gliding range of 8 to 10 miles. Normally gliders are never released directly over the objective but at a sufficient distance so that towing aircraft need not fly over the point of attack.

While the Germans were apparently successful in glider operations in Belgium [in the comparatively small (but important) operation at Fort Eben Emael], the glider performance in Crete resulted in many casualties due to premature release, short turns, navigation errors, and rocky terrain. The troop glider, like all aircraft, is extremely vulnerable to small-arms fire when gliding low near ground defenses. Although it is not clear how light tanks if brought by air would be employed, it is believed that gliderborne units are not equipped to follow up tank advance, at least in the early stages.

They lack motor transport and are, therefore, not mobile. Darkness is also a deterrent to gliderborne operations. So far as is known, glider attacks have been limited to dawn and dusk operations.

When a glider attack is made a part of large-scale airborne operations, it is important that glider airdromes should not be located too near the objective, since concentrations of aircraft are conspicuous and likely to receive attention from hostile aircraft before the units get on their way. It is, on the other hand, impracticable to conduct glider attacks from airdromes more than 200 miles away. Over longer distances, decisions at the rear take progressively longer to affect the action and thus make operation more difficult for the pilots. Furthermore, it is desirable that troops going into action not be kept seated in aircraft for longer than 2 or 3 hours, the time required for the 200-mile flight. Finally, since dawn is the usual time of attack, and such attacks cannot be made unless the planes take off at night, it would follow that they should depart early in the day and not spend too much time on the journey.

# GERMAN MOTORCYCLE TRACTOR

## Tactical and Technical Trends, No. 19, February 25, 1943

The invasion of Crete revealed for the first time the use by the Germans of the motorcycle tractor for the purpose of hauling light, single-axle, open trailers or light guns. This tractor is known to be employed in the Middle East and, according to recent newspaper accounts, it is now to be seen on the Eastern Front. It is a suitable vehicle for accompanying airborne troops. Early in 1941, it was accepted as an army vehicle and received the number Sd.Kfz. 2 (Sonder Kraftfahrzug - special motor vehicle).

### a. Body

The accompanying sketches show that the body (1) is a box-like structure made of pressed metal in two halves, and joined along a horizontal plane below the track-guards (2). It contains the driving position (3), the engine (4) and transmission, and a transverse seat (5) at the rear over the cooling system (6). The

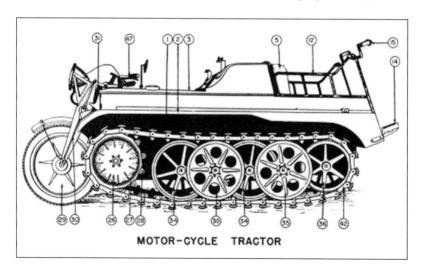

MOTOR-CYCLE TRACTOR

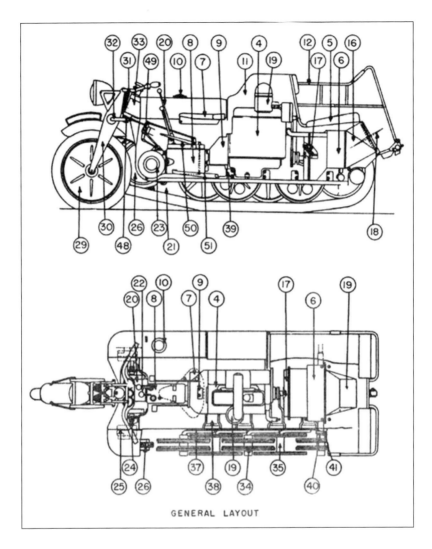

GENERAL LAYOUT

driver is seated on a saddle (7) mounted above the gearbox (8) and clutch housing (9), and has two rubber knee-pads fitted beneath the dashboard. On each side, the track-guards carry gasoline tanks (10) at the front while, level with the engine, the sides are built up (11) and contain on the left the tool kit and on the right the battery and fuze panel.

At each side of the passenger seat there is a light rail (12), while foot rests, rifle rests (14), and clips (15) are provided at the rear.

## b. Engine

The power unit (4) is an Opel "Olympia model 38," gasoline engine, mounted towards the rear of the body. It is a four-cycle, four-cylinder unit developing about 36 brake horse power at 3,400 rpm.

- Bore - 80 mm
- Stroke - 76 mm
- Engine capacity - 1,478 cc
- Compression ratio - 6
- Firing order - 1 - 3 - 4 - 2

The engine body is in two main parts: the cylinder head, and the cylinder block and crankcase (both in one piece).

## c. Crankshaft Assembly

This is supported in four main bearings. The pistons are of light metal and are fitted with two compression and one oil-scraper rings. The wrist or piston pins are full floating and are prevented from sideward movement by locking rings on each side.

## d. Valve Operation

The overhead valves (one intake and one exhaust for each cylinder) are operated by pushrods and rockers from the camshaft, which is mounted in four bearings in the crankcase. The gasoline pump, tachometer, oil pump, and distributor are all driven from the camshaft.

- Valve clearance (warm) Intake - 0.2 mm (8/1000 in)
- Valve clearance (warm) Exhaust - 0.3 mm (12/1000 in)

## e. Cooling

An impeller-type water pump, together with the generator, is driven from a master pulley on the free end of the crankshaft and circulates water between the engine and the radiator (6), which is located at the rear of the vehicle. A small water tank is mounted above the pump. The laminated radiator is built in a large airduct (16), in which there is a fan (17) driven direct from the crankshaft. The rear end of the airduct may be closed by a flap (18) operated by a hand lever on the left of the driver.

## f. Lubrication

Oil is pressure-circulated by a gear pump from the sump through a strainer and passes through the bearings of the crankshaft, connecting rods, camshaft, tappets, and valve rockers at a pressure of 30 to 45 pounds per square inch. Piston pins and cylinder walls are splash-lubricated.

In order that the oil pressure may not rise too high, there is an excess-pressure valve in the wall of the oil pump, and this returns some of the oil to the sump.

An oil cleaner of the metal-disk type is fitted. This is itself cleaned by turning the ratchet on the top.

## g. Fuel-Supply

An Opel downdraft carburetor, with a large oil-bath-type air filter (19) on the air intake, is fitted. Gas is drawn from the tanks (of which there are two, each holding 5.5 U.S. gallons) and fed to the carburetor by a mechanical diaphragm pump of normal design, which is driven from the camshaft.

## h. Electrical Equipment

Ignition is by Bosch coil and distributor, the latter being driven from the camshaft. A Bosch 75-watt generator, with voltage regulator, is mounted on the right side of the engine and together with the water pump is driven by a V-belt from the master pulley. A Bosch starter motor is also fitted on the right side. The 6-volt battery is mounted on the right side above the track-guard.

## i. Starting Equipment

Normally the engine is started by a self-starter controlled by a pull-knob on the dashboard. A crank is also provided and, for use, is inserted in an opening in the radiator grill at the back of the vehicle (just above the trailer coupling) and pushed through to engage with the crankshaft.

## j. Transmission

Transmission is through an Opel multiple-spring, single dry-plate clutch, mounted on the flywheel, to a 3-speed-and-reverse gearbox (8), which also incorporates an auxiliary gear box, giving high and low ratios so that in effect 6 forward speeds may be obtained. A long gear-shift lever (20), held near the top in a gate (the H-shaped aperture in which the gear lever operates) on the dashboard in front of the driver, gives the main gear selection, while a shorter lever (21), to the rear of the first, gives selection of high and low ratios for road or cross-country travel. A hinged latch which covers the "reverse" part of the gate prevents accidental engaging of that gear, while an extension of the latch beyond the hinge makes its removal an easy matter.

The vehicle must be stationary while changing ratio in the auxiliary gearbox.

The speedometer is driven from the gearbox.

## k. Differential

The differential (22) is of the controlled spur-gear type and incorporates two steering brakes (23), one for each track. These are internal expanding, and in order to increase their braking efficiency the drums are not directly fastened to the axle shafts, but are driven at considerably greater speed from the differential spur pinions through a set of gears.

## l. Sprocket

From the differential, the drive passes through the steering brakes (23) and metal couplings (24) to the final reduction gears (25), and thence to the sprockets (26). Each sprocket is a narrow twin-rimmed wheel, of which the inner and outer rims are shod with rubber pads (27) (12 per rim) to form a continuous tire. The pads have the same inside curvature as the rim, but are flat outside. Adjustable rollers (28) (12 per sprocket) are fitted between the rims to act as teeth and to engage the track. An internal expanding brake, which is foot operated, is mounted inside each sprocket.

## m. Suspension

*(1) Front Wheel*

The front wheel (29) is a pressed-steel disk type with a 3.5- by 19-inch tire (tire pressure 34 lbs. per sq. in.) and mounted in a pressed steel, motorcycle front-wheel fork (30) of conventional pattern. The springing (two vertical coil springs) (31), with controllable friction-disk shock absorbers (32), and the steering column (33) are very similar to those of a normal motorcycle.

*(2) Track Assembly*

The track assembly, which is of the usual type for half-track vehicles, consists on each side of a driving sprocket (26), four equal size, double-rimmed bogie wheels (34 and 35), and an idler wheel (36). Of the bogie wheels, the odd numbers (34) (from the front) are narrow wheels with radial spokes, while the even numbers are wider, pressed-steel disk wheels. The former run between the rims of the latter, the whole bogie and idler system being set rim to axle.

The bogie wheels are mounted on bell cranks (37) fastened to torsion bars, which pass across the body of the vehicle in crosstubes (33) of circular section and are anchored in the opposite side. The torsion bars of the corresponding bogie wheels of the two sides are carried one above the other (39) in the same cross tube.

The idler is simply another narrow-rimmed bogie wheel and is carried on an eccentric arm (40) which can be adjusted by a screw rod (41) passing through a bracket on the body. By this means the position of the idler can be varied, and hence the track tension may be adjusted. The bogie and idler wheel rims have thin, solid rubber tires. There are no return rollers, the track returning along the tops of the bogie wheels.

**n. Track**

Each track is made up of 40 forged steel links (42) (fig. 1) joined together by a bolt (43). These link joints are lubricated from oil chambers (44) which also, in part, form the tongues of the track links and pass between the rims of the bogie wheels. Above the oil chambers and track bolts, rubber shoes (45) are mounted.

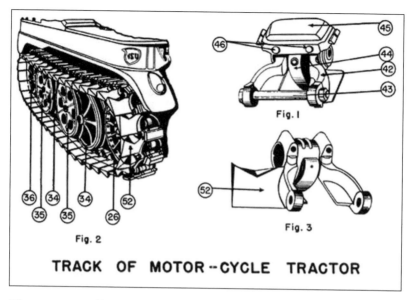

Fig. I

Fig. 3

Fig. 2

## TRACK OF MOTOR-CYCLE TRACTOR

These are easily replaceable, being retained by 4 screws (46) only.

### o. Steering

The motorcycle tractor is steered by the front wheel, by handlebars (47) in the normal manner of a motorcycle, and for sharp turns, by the steering brakes, operating on the tracks.

Two take-off rings (48) at the bottom of the steering column are connected by rods to arms on the brake crosstube (49). These in turn actuate levers, the ends of which are joined by means of adjustable rods to the steering brakes (23).

The steering brakes come into play for turns of over 5°, corresponding to a movement in either direction of about 1 3/4 inches at the ends of the handlebars.

### p. Brakes

The footbrake, which is located on the right, and the handbrake (50) both operate an internal expanding brake mounted in each sprocket.

### q. Driver's Controls and Instruments

These consist of the following:-

(1) steering handlebars with right hand throttle twist grip;

(2) main and auxiliary gear selection levers;

(3) a footpedal (51) on the left, operating the clutch;

(4) a handbrake (50) mounted on the left of the gearbox cover;

(5) a footbrake on the right;

(6) a radiator shutter control on the inside of the body, left of the driver, -

together with starter button, ignition and lighting switches, tachometer, speedometer, odometer, oil-pressure gauge, and water-temperature gauge.

### r. Modifications for Tropical Use

A German document details several modifications which are made to the motorcycle tractor to fit it for use under tropical conditions.

*(1) Engine*

The oil filler cap has a linen hood tied over it, and the breather pipe has a steel-wool filter held between two pins near the bottom. For cleaning purposes, the filter may be removed after the lower pin has been extracted.

*(2) Cooling*

In order to provide sufficient cooling, the fan is driven at 1.4 times the crankshaft speed.

*(3) Fuel Supply*

The Opel carburetor is replaced by a Solex model, believed to be of the duplex downdraft type. A filter is incorporated between the gas tanks and the pump.

*(4) Air Filter*

The "Knecht Tornado" air filter fitted to the normal vehicle is replaced by a similar type of oilbath filter, incorporating a mechanical precipitator on the inlet side.

*(5) Electrical Equipment*

A new generator is fitted, while a solenoid-operated starter motor replaces the mechanically-operated type fitted in the normal model. The starter push button is located on the right side of the body level with the driver's seat. The distributor is enveloped in a linen bag.

*(6) Transmission*

Both main and auxiliary gear levers have linen hoods tied to them to cover their points of entry into the gearboxes. The breather holes in the gearboxes, the steering brakes, and the stub axle housings are all covered with cloth hoods.

*(7) Tracks*

For special purposes, tracks in which the links have extension plates (52) welded to their outside (figs. 2 & 3) are provided. These are probably for use in very loose sand or swampy ground.

*(8) Brakes*

The covers of the track brakes have extension plates welded to the upper halves to prevent the entry of sand as much as possible.

*(9) Controls*

The throttle twist grip is covered with a linen sheath which is tied to the grip at each end and to the handlebars, with sufficient free cloth allowed between these fastenings to permit full movement of the twist grip.

*(10) Additional Equipment*

A 0.4-gallon container for distilled water, and a gallon tank for radiator water are fitted.

A length of wire (16 to 20 feet) and a 13- by 16-foot tarpaulin complete the special tropical equipment of the motorcycle tractor.

## s. Further Particulars

*(1) Dimensions*

- Length, over-all: 9 ft 0 in
- Width, over-all: 3 ft 3 in
- Height, over-all: 3 ft 11 in
- Width between tracks: 2 ft 8 in
- Wheelbase, from center of front wheel to center of track: 4 ft 5 in
- Length of track in contact with ground: 2 ft 8 in
- Belly clearance: 9 in

*(2) Weight*
- Without load: 2,690 lbs
- Loaded: 3,470 lbs
- Axle load, front wheel: 120 lbs
- Load on tracks: 3,248 lbs
- (3) Performance
- Maximum speed on roads at 3,000 rpm: 38 mph
- Maximum speed on roads at 4,000 rpm: 51 mph*
- Trailer capacity: 1/2 ton (approx)
- Maximum gradient, loose sand without trailer: 24° (45% or 1 in 2.25)
- Maximum gradient, loose sand with trailer: 12° (20% or 1 in 5)
- Depth of water forded: 1 ft 7 in
- Fuel capacity: 9 gal
- Gasoline consumption on roads: 17 mpg
- Gasoline consumption cross-country (approx): 12 mpg

*\* This speed, it is stated, is only to be attempted in exceptional circumstances.*

# AIRBORNE RECOILLESS GUNS

## *Handbook on German Military Forces*

### a. 75-MM AIRBORNE RECOILLESS GUN (7.5 cm L. G. 40).

### (1) General description.

The 7.5 cm L. G. 40, formerly known as the 7.5 cm L. G. 1 (L) Rh., needs no recoil mechanism. The breech is designed to eliminate recoil by emitting part of the propellent gases to the rear. Weight has been reduced considerably by constructing the carriage largely of light alloys, and the gun may be dropped by parachute in two wicker containers. The thin horizontal sliding breechblock is hand-operated. A Venturi tube extends from the rear of the breech which is bored to allow gases to escape. Light metal disk-type wheels are fitted to the mount.

### (2) Characteristics.

* Caliber: 75 mm (2.95 inches).

*A 75mm Airborne Recoilless Gun (7.5 cm L. G. 40) needed no recoil mechanism producing a lightweight weapon which could be air-dropped.*

- Length of tube including breech ring and jet: 45.28 inches.
- Weight in action: 321 pounds.
- Maximum range (HE): 8,900 yards (estimated).
- Muzzle velocity (HE): 1,238 feet per second.
- Traverse with elevation -15° to +42°: 30° right and left.
- Traverse with elevation -15° to +20°: 360° right and left.
- Elevation with traverse of 360°: -15° to +20°.
- Elevation with traverse of 30°, right and left: -15° to + 42°.
- Traction: Airborne.

**(3) Ammunition.**

HE, APCBC, and hollow-charge projectiles are fired. Projectile weights are: HE, 12 pounds, APCBC, 15 pounds; hollow charge, 10.13 pounds. The hollow-charge projectile will penetrate 50 mm at 30 degrees from normal.

### b. 105-MM AIRBORNE RECOILLESS GUN (10.5 cm L. G. 40).

**(1) General description.**

The 10.5 cm L. G. 40, formerly known as the 10.5 cm L. G. 2 Kp., like the 7.5 cm L. G. 40, has a jet at the rear for the escape of part of the propellent gases instead of a recoil system. There is no breechblock. The firing mechanism is operated from the top of the breech ring and the striker hits a primer in the side of the cartridge. A modification of this weapon, the 10.5 cm L. G. 40/2, also exists.

**(2) Characteristics.**

- Caliber: 105 mm (4.14 inches).
- Length of tube, including jet: 6 feet, 3 inches.
- Weight in action: 855 pounds.
- Maximum range: 8,694 yards.
- Muzzle velocity (HE): 1,099 feet per second.
- Traverse: 80°.
- Elevation: -15° to +40° 30'.
- Traction: Airborne.

**(3) Ammunition.**

HE and hollow-charge projectiles are fired. The base of the cartridge case has a circular Bakelite disk which is destroyed when the gun fires. Projectile weights are: HE, 32.63 pounds; hollow charge, 25.88 pounds.

## c. 105-MM AIRBORNE RECOILLESS GUN (10.5 cm L. G. 42).

### (1) General description.

The 10.5 cm L. G. 42, formerly known as the L. G. 2 Rh, differs from the 10.5 cm L. G. 40 in that it has a horizontal sliding breechblock bored for the passage of gases to the rear. The mount is made of fairly heavy tubing, and is designed for rapid dismantling and reassembly. Both air and pack transport are possible. A variation, known as 10.5 cm L. G. 42/1, differs in weight (1,191 pounds). It uses the same range tables.

### (2) Characteristics.

- Caliber: 105 mm (4.14 inches).
- Length of tube: 6 feet, 0.28 inch (including jet).
- Weight in action: 1,217 pounds.
- Maximum range (HE): 8,695 yards.
- Muzzle velocity: 1,099 feet per second.
- Traverse: 360° at elevations up to 12°; 71° 15' at elevations over 12°.
- Elevation: 15° to 42° 35'.
- Traction: Airborne or pack.

### (3) Ammunition.

This weapon fires HE, hollow-charge, smoke, and HE incendiary projectiles. The projectile weights are: HE, 32.58 pounds: hollow charge, 26.62 and 27.17 pounds; smoke, 32.36 pounds; and HE incendiary, 33.52 pounds.

# More from the same series

Most books from the 'Hitler's War Machine' series are edited and endorsed by Emmy Award winning film maker and military historian Bob Carruthers, producer of Discovery Channel's Line of Fire and Weapons of War and BBC's Both Sides of the Line. Long experience and strong editorial control gives the military history enthusiast the ability to buy with confidence.

| | | | |
|---|---|---|---|
| Tiger I in Combat | Tiger I Crew Manual | Panzers at War 1939-1942 | Panzers at War 1943-1945 |
| Wolf Pack - the U boats | Poland 1939 | Luftwaffe Combat Reports | Eastern Front Night |
| Eastern Front Encirclement | Panzer Combat Reports | The Panther V in Combat | German Tank Hunters |
| The Afrika Korps in Combat | Panzers I & II | Panzer III | Panzer IV |

*For more information visit www.pen-and-sword.co.uk*